# THE FIRE OF THE HEART

## True Meditation as a Direct Doorway to Spiritual Awakening

## PETER BAMPTON

**ISBN** 978-1-64606-769-5

Published and distributed by Awakened Life Publishing.
Printed by Lulu Press, Inc.

Awakened Life Project®

Dedicated to all my Teachers and students past, present and future

# Contents

.

# Foreword

## By Pedro Morais

My first contact with the book you hold in your hands happened at one of those times when we are overwhelmed by the absolute certainty that everything makes sense, that everything is right and that life continually gives us what we need most in every moment.

This book was given to me by Peter Bampton, my spiritual teacher, spiritual brother and great friend, during a solitary one-month retreat that I did at Quinta da Mizarela, the ashram of The Awakened Life Project in the mountains of Central Portugal. I remember that day vividly. It was at the beginning of the second week of the retreat. I had already done countless meditation retreats, but for the first time I had the feeling that I was at risk, that I had no teacher to guide me on this journey and I remember the fear and, at the same time, the sense of potential this evoked in me. A few hours later, that same day, after lunch, Pete walked past me and gave me his book saying, "It's for you." As I sat in silence, I did not look into his eyes or utter a word, but inwardly I thanked him deeply for knowing that the guide was there for the next three weeks of retreat.

Reading this book during that solitary retreat was literally a catalyst for a radical expansion of consciousness. In giving up control and letting myself be led by what I was reading I had access to a channel of knowledge that brought me to a growing understanding of what Reality really is. This came to me through two processes that happened internally and simultaneously. On one hand the book had the power to reflect, with the precision of a mirror, the operating system from which human conditionings arise and the consequent procession of events that make up the whole "personal drama of our lives". And on the other hand, it functioned as a precise map that informed each step and every challenge that anyone who has a genuine interest and passion for the Awakening Process will inevitably face in the course of their journey.

The content of *The Fire of the Heart* goes far beyond a profound teaching and exploration of meditation. This book is an invitation that invites the reader to take a journey into the discovery of his or her True Nature. Through Peter's guidance and exploration the practice of True Meditation comes alive not only in the time we spend sitting on the cushion, but in a continuous act of courageous transcendence of apparent limitations, an embrace of the Fullness of who we really *are*, at every moment and in every circumstance.

Who am I? Who am I *really*? Why am I here? What is my purpose in this life? Reading this book invites you into a consistent contemplation of these questions, making clear that the art of living an Awakened Life is closely related to the capacity to embrace these questions, while resisting the temptation to need to find a definitive answer to them.

I have the utmost respect and gratitude for Peter, for his continued commitment to initiate and lead in what it means to "live in the unknown" and to be an example of surrender, trust, and humility that inspires, invites and opens the way to the emergence of an individual and collective Awakening. And so I am honoured to write the foreword to this book in which Peter summarizes so clearly, simply and profoundly the teachings and vision of the Awakened Life Project, which is the fruit of his long experience and untiring dedication to the creation of a new culture rooted in the truth of non-duality.

If you are one of those rare human beings who is interested in radical awakening and transformation, who wants to genuinely discover what it means to be a free human being, who is willing to take full responsibility for their own happiness and live for a greater purpose, then fasten your seatbelt now for the journey of a lifetime is about to begin.

Pedro Morais

Sintra, Portugal
2019

*The truth was obscure,*
*too profound and too pure;*
*to live it you have to explode.*


Bob Dylan

# Introduction

The *Fire of the Heart* is a distillation of all that I have learned about the Awakening Process up to this point in time. And, as inspired as I am by the task of sharing what I have learned, I have to begin by saying that all my explanations will inevitably fall short, because only an infinite explanation could possibly capture the mystery of Awakening. You will not find that infinite explanation in this book but if my words succeed in igniting a spark of the Infinite within you, and if that spark finds fertile ground to take root in your Heart, then my intent in writing this book will have been more than fulfilled. If you are new to meditation and the idea of Spiritual Awakening it is my hope that this book will inspire you to set sail upon the wide sunlit seas of the Great Way. And if you are well on your Way, it is my hope that *The Fire of the Heart* will further enrich and deepen your journey.

I decided to call this book *The Fire of the Heart* because when I contemplate that mysterious, captivating Presence that has always been the consistent thread guiding me further and deeper, I envisage it as a Sacred Fire of purifying Heat and liberating Light. As I am sure you will appreciate as you read, *The Fire of the Heart* is a perfect metaphor for the purifying alchemy of the Awakening Process that I am going to share with you.

Those of you who know me personally know that I am a rebel at heart and have never craved the trappings of the world. My journey of Awakening began in my early teenage years when I found no resonance with the Catholic Christianity of my upbringing and only boredom in the mundane routines of school. Besides immersing myself every evening after school in learning how to play guitar by listening to and emulating the music of my rock heroes, the only other outlet for my adolescent rebellion and growing sense of aloneness was when I took long walks every Sunday into the countryside surrounding the town where I grew up in Hertfordshire, England. On these walks, as I rambled amongst the fields, hills and woods, I immediately felt an enormous sense of relief and all my frustrations would be washed away. Then, at some point on my walk, I would find a peaceful, secluded spot with a tree branch or rusty piece of farming equipment to sit down on and then it would happen.

The "it" that would happen is much of what this book is about. I had no idea what it was back then, but now I would call it "spontaneous meditation". I would simply sit, at first with my eyes open, gazing vacantly at whatever scene was before me, and gradually my inner subjective sense of "I" would dissolve. By that I mean that the usual continuous activity of thinking slowed down and fell away from the foreground of my experience. Sometimes it would disappear altogether. I would find myself immersed in an utterly captivating depth and silence. Sitting like this, there was no labeling or interpretation of what I was seeing or experiencing. Sometimes everything appeared to be shining with a translucent light and I would momentarily lose all sense of boundaries and merge into my surroundings. Then, eventually my eyes would close and I would have the sensation of falling into a bottomless well of black nothingness and deep peace. At times the peace would become so profound that I could not move and I would lose track of time completely. I had no idea what was happening. All I knew was that I was being spontaneously magnetized by a Mystery that I could not understand.

As I mentioned I found no resonance with the Catholic Christianity of my upbringing. I already found going to Mass interminably boring and was simply going through the motions. I would silently endure the ordeal, sitting in the last pew at the back of the church. I could not bring myself to recite any longer, "I believe in One God, the Father, the Almighty, Maker of Heaven and Earth..." The idea of a Creator God who was some kind of distant Parental Deity that could be contacted through unquestioning belief and prayer seemed a very dubious presumption to my adolescent mind.

The last Mass I ever attended was on a Saturday evening when I was fourteen years old. The bells signifying the end of the silent period of prayer after Holy Communion had not been rung after what seemed like an unusually long time. When I looked up to see why I saw that the priest had dozed off in his chair! At first I found this amusing as I could see one of my friends, who was the altar boy, surreptitiously trying to nudge him awake, but then a flash of rebellion suddenly overwhelmed me. All of my submerged frustration at having been inoculated all my life into what I perceived to be an empty farce of religiosity exploded within me. I knew in that moment that it was all over.

I got up abruptly and walked out of the church. I vividly remember the moment I opened and walked through the huge heavy wooden door. It was a decisive moment of Pure Freedom. I felt as if I was throwing off a huge weight that I had not even known that I was carrying. I walked home at a brisk pace through the drizzling rain possessed by a concentrated determination.

The following Sunday morning I went out for my regular walk. I sat down upon a hill overlooking my hometown and, as I gazed down at the array of houses, roads, cars and gardens below, the silence and depth descended upon me once more. Overcome by a profound peace and sense of liberating detachment from everything that appeared before me, I had a tacit recognition that I did not belong to this world as it was commonly conceived, that what people generally valued and were living for held no interest for me whatsoever. Immersed in this powerful Presence that seemed to be lifting me out of the world, I remember a very clear thought arising spontaneously that had the force of an inner declaration: "I will never live a mediocre life. I would rather die." That moment made a very deep impression on me. When I finally got up to walk back home for lunch, I had absolutely no idea what it meant or what I would do or wanted to do, I simply felt a deep sense of conviction and a light bubbling joy.

Reflecting back on it now, I can see that what occurred during that weekend was really the beginning of my spiritual path. A movement of surrender had occurred, but it was not fully conscious yet. Somehow a shift was catalyzed by that decisive moment when I walked out of church. That shift was both a pivotal step in my individuation, a growth into a greater sense of freethinking autonomy, and the next morning on the hill I was opened to a Mystery that completely transcended my individuality. For the first time I became intuitively aware that the Presence that had been engulfing me when I sat down alone in nature was not something "other" than me that was somehow "descending" from outside myself. Rather that Presence that was beyond my comprehension was the deepest essence of my Being and was therefore what I could trust more deeply than anything or anyone else. And here I am typing these words forty years later still captivated by that Presence that is beyond my comprehension.

Later in my twenties I discovered Buddhism and was immediately drawn to the idea of a Spiritual Enlightenment that was not based on belief but on meditation and inquiry. From that point on the practice of meditation provided me with an ongoing thread of connection to this Presence. While traveling in Thailand I did my first silent meditation retreat that lasted for ten days and was held in a Buddhist forest monastery. This experience changed the orientation of my life forever. Meditating eighteen hours a day I was quickly drawn into profound depths of peace and bliss. Toward the end of the retreat I got up from my meditation cushion and walked out into the surrounding forest and a radical shift in my perception occurred. Overwhelmed by wonder and ecstasy, I was literally liberated from any sense of separation from my surroundings. The jungle was teeming with life; birds were cackling in the towering trees, long processions of enormous ants were crawling past my feet, the buzzing of all kinds of insects filled the air, and it was all "Me". Whoever "I" was had somehow become untethered from my usual experience of being a body and mind called Peter. I now experienced myself to be a vast, limitless expanse that was non-separate from everything and yet was radically free from everything. From that day until the end of the retreat I would dissolve into deep bliss during the meditations and walk ecstatically along the forest paths during the breaks, overwhelmed by this thrilling luminous recognition that I had no words for.

Looking back in the light of my current understanding it is clear that what occurred in the forest monastery in Thailand was my first Awakening to the radical, inconceivable Truth of Non-Duality (or in Buddhist terminology a glimpse of Nirvana or Enlightenment), in which the apparent division of experience into subject and object, the perceiver and the perceived was dissolved. That penetrating clarity and tremendous liberation soon faded, but from then on I was haunted by it and I could never forget it and my life became more and more oriented around seeking for the rediscovery of that Awakening. Whenever I was alone I was drawn into what felt like a silent, magnetic Fire that had ignited deep within my Heart in that forest in Thailand. And so I continued to meditate and my longing to merge with that mysterious, captivating Fire continued to grow and to overwhelm all my other desires and interests.

Through surrendering to that longing of *The Fire of the Heart* I discovered a source of guidance that has since led me on a miraculous journey – to Masters and Teachers whose profound wisdom, blazing Light and Grace has illumined the Way and into meditation retreats and communities of spiritual fellowship and practice that have been invaluable crucibles of learning, purification and Realization.

Because meditation has been at the very core of my own odyssey of Awakening, at first unconsciously and then consciously, I have felt immensely inspired to share what I have discovered about meditation in a way that frees the practice from many common misunderstandings and traditional cultural baggage. And so ten years ago I began to teach meditation retreats as part of the offering of The Awakened Life Project, an initiative that I co-founded with my wife, Cynthia, in the mountains of Central Portugal in 2007.

Since that time many people have asked me if I had a book available that would guide them further in deepening their practice. Also over the years The Awakened Life Project has developed into a vibrant and thriving spiritual network of committed participants and I have increasingly felt the necessity to write a book that could be a "source text" for people involved in our shared experiment in creating a culture based on the Non-Dual Truth of our Prior Unity. So I began writing this book in 2014 and finished a trial version that I self-published for the benefit of people involved with our Project in mid 2016. I was far from happy with it though and so I continued writing on and off until the process hit a yearlong hiatus after we suffered a devastating fire in 2017 at Quinta da Mizarela, our home and the ashram of The Awakened Life Project.

The nagging voice to continue the book haunted me until I surrendered and I began working on the book again during the winter of 2018-2019 in a rented cottage outside Tiruvannamalai, South India. This was not only an important focused time to write the book but I also found myself on an ever-deepening journey of Awakening in doing so. While in India I was joyfully immersed in the "blessing field" of the sacred ancient mountain of Arunachala, regarded as a literal manifestation of Lord Shiva in Hindu Vedanta, and the ashram and caves of the greatest Indian sage of the twentieth century, Ramana Maharshi, where I would usually meditate for several hours in the mornings. And so, carried on the wings of the palpable Grace of Arunachala and Ramana Maharshi I experienced a flow of writing like never before. So much more poured out of me than I had originally envisaged and as this was happening it became clear that I was also writing for a potentially wider audience and so I have decided to publish this book.

As you read this book I encourage you to open yourself to wonder, to mystery, to new possibilities. If there is one thing I have learned it is that a mind filled with prejudices, concepts, theories and scriptures is not capable of genuine learning. To learn we have to be willing to unlearn first and the Awakening Process is primarily a process of unlearning, of letting go of all that we have accumulated. So I encourage you to suspend your habitual presumptions about the nature of Life and Consciousness, even if you have been on the Path for many years, and stay open and receptive to whatever resonates with your deepest intuition as you read. My intent is not to convince you of anything but to invite you into an open-ended journey of Self-Discovery.

To facilitate this process I have interspersed the text with the symbol *****. When you come upon this symbol I encourage you to pause for a few minutes or more to absorb and quietly consider what you have just read. Resist the temptation to read too quickly in an effort to acquire knowledge and take the time to allow whatever resonates intuitively to percolate through your being.

I hope this book will be of some help to you on your journey and that it will inspire you to dive ever deeper into your True Self, to the point that any other idea of "self" organically falls away.

Peter Bampton

Quinta da Mizarela
Benfeita
Portugal
2019

# Acknowledgements

Very deep gratitude to my dear wife Cynthia for her excellent copy editing skills and suggestions and for supporting me with the space and time needed to write this book in the midst of a busy, engaged life co-leading The Awakened Life Project.

Thank you to my dear students and friends – brothers and sisters of The Awakened Life Project – for their dedication to the Awakening Process and for inspiring me to write.

Thank you to Nico Fernandes for his creative book design.

Thank you to Natacha Leite for the layout and typesetting.

*****

A deep bow to the Masters and Teachers along the Way who have had a profound impact on my Awakening Process and without whom this book would not have been written...

Gautama Buddha for pointing out the Way.

Sri Nisagardatta Maharaj for being the first to show me I AM THAT!

Andrew Cohen for pouring gasoline on the Fire of my Heart and being a radical pioneer of unimaginable possibilities.

Peter Ragnar for being such a Roaring Lion and teaching me that "what you set is what you get".

Ramana Maharshi for the overwhelming Benediction of His Grace.

Avatar Adi Da Samraj for the immeasurable Gift of Radical Understanding, His peerless "full-spectrum" Completion of the Great Tradition and for continuing to "kick ass" from behind the veil. I am Forever at Your Feet.

# Part I

# THE GREAT SEARCH

# Chapter 1

# The Great Search

WHETHER we are rich or poor, young or old, male or female, British, Portuguese, American or Russian, we all experience an irrepressible longing for True Happiness, True Peace, True Freedom, and True Fulfillment. This profound urge, which seems to be inseparable from our embodiment as human beings, propels us into the world of experience and shapes our individual and collective destiny.

If we closely inspect our experience we will see that more or less everything that we do through the means of body, speech and mind is driven by this fundamental desire to be Happy, Free and Fulfilled. Through the acquisition of various objects, relationships and activities we are constantly seeking pleasure and security while attempting to avoid pain and insecurity. Even when we are motivated to help make other people happy, we want them to be happy because seeing them happy makes us feel happy. Indeed, even if we sacrifice our own comfort to help others, and so experience some form of suffering as a result, we then experience a contentment that transcends our own suffering because it makes us happy to care for those others regardless of our own discomfort.

Therefore whether we look at our most selfishly motivated desires or our most altruistically motivated desires we will see that the driving force of our existence is to *become Happy* and through that Happiness to experience enduring Peace and Fulfillment. But do we ever truly, fundamentally and consistently *become* Happy? Have *you* discovered a lasting Happiness, a deep Peace and an overflowing sense of Fulfillment that is not dependent on any particular experience, relationship or activity?

If we are honest with ourselves almost all of us will be forced to acknowledge that despite the various joys, pleasures and consolations we may have experienced and do experience in the course of our lives, we have yet to discover True Happiness, True Peace, True Freedom and True Fulfillment. How can we know this for ourselves? Simply by honestly asking the question: am I still *seeking* Happiness, Peace, Freedom and Fulfillment? If the answer is yes, then what I am saying above may be true.

It may be a hard truth to swallow but all of our *seeking* for Happiness is based on our *presumption* of unhappiness. All of our seeking for Fulfillment is based on our presumption that we are already less than full. We presume that Happiness, Peace, Freedom and Fulfillment are not yet the case and so they must be pursued and achieved. Something is necessary, some form of action, some object, some "other". But this incessant movement of seeking never reaches its goal. Indeed, it is the activity of *seeking* Happiness, Peace, Freedom and Fulfillment, this almost continuous arising of desire, of wanting this and avoiding that,

that keeps us in a state of almost constant discontent and unhappiness.

No doubt you have observed in your own experience that when your energy and attention are outwardly focused on the material and emotional domains of existence, on what you want or do not want, then your tendency is to be endlessly lost in thought and emotional reactivity. When you are lost in desiring what is *not* here and now or in resisting what *is* here and now, you tend to be constantly preoccupied with the problems and difficulties of daily life and at the mercy of random emotional impulses and physical cravings of all kinds. Is this not true in your own experience?

When this Great Search for True Happiness, Peace, Freedom and Fulfillment is driving us through each day, we generally live a discontented, restless, and victimized life, punctuated by moments or periods of relative happiness and peace when we appear to get what we want or what we think we need. When a desire arises and agitates our mind our inherent happiness is obscured and hence we feel restless and unhappy until that desire is fulfilled. In those moments or periods when our desires are fulfilled the seeking mind dissolves in temporary relief from the tension of the search and thus we temporarily enjoy the True Happiness and Fulfillment of our innate True Nature. But then, because we mistakenly believe that the source of our momentary or periodic happiness lies in the acquisition of objects, activities or others "out there", even when we do get what we want or what we think we need for a moment or period of time, we soon find ourselves wanting or resisting again. Inevitably when the excitation and satiation of experiencing the fulfillment of our desire begins to fade we are left high and dry once more with our basic discontent. Even when we are happiest this basic discontent can still be there as an often nagging background sense that our present happiness will not last, because we know that it is not possible to continuously sustain a high and happy feeling or the pleasing circumstances in which we may temporarily find ourselves. If we bring some sensitivity and intelligence to bear on our experience of desire and seeking it soon becomes obvious that the objects of our desire never quench the fire of our desire. Indeed, trying to quench the fire of our desires by fulfilling them is like trying to quench a fire by pouring petrol on it. Our desires and fears, likes and dislikes, all agitate and impel the activity of our mind to the peaks of its intensity and it is our addiction to this agitation and excitement that obscures our inherent happiness and eventually makes us feel discontented. When the agitated activity of mind becomes less intense, we feel calmer and more content, and hence we are able to experience more clearly our innate Happiness. Looked at closely then, we can recognize that desire and fear are in fact two aspects of the same thing. By desiring whatever seems to contribute to our happiness, we will inevitably fear whatever objects, activities and relationships appear to detract from our happiness.

*****

I am sure we would all agree that for every pleasurable experience in life there is at least an equally painful one and that much of our day-to-day life as a human being in this world is a rather neutral matter of maintaining our functional existence. If we slow down a little bit and simply observe the highs and lows that constitute the flow of our psychophysical experience it soon becomes clear that the only constant in life is change itself. Everything that appears in our lives externally in the world "out there" or psychologically in the world "in here" is in perpetual flux. Every object, every other, every thought, every emotion, is appearing and disappearing, is fluid and ultimately ungraspable and uncontrollable. Trying to find security and solace in the ever-changing forms of conditional experience is like trying to catch water in our hand. Hence the Great Search for fulfillment in the realms of the body, mind and world keeps us in a state of restless seeking and dissatisfaction with very little deep relief.

If we widen the scope of our inquiry and consider the human condition as a whole, we will see that this insatiable Great Search for True Happiness, Peace, Freedom and Fulfillment, is the root cause of not only our individual, but also our collective, suffering, degeneration and destruction as a race. We begin to see and understand directly why the human-created world tends to be such a cruel, exploitative and dishonest place, compared with the beauty and integrity of the Earth. We begin to see and to feel that the insatiable craving and discontent that drives this Great Search is a form of psychic possession that, like a parasite, drains our vital resources, just as the ego-constructed "civilized" world is exhausting the Earth's resources.

# Chapter 2

# Growing Up

Before I venture further into our exploration of the Great Search, I first want to provide some context by inviting you to join me in taking a wide-angle view of our shared trajectory through this mysterious phenomenon called Life. One of the most important things I have learned and continue to learn is that context is everything, especially when we are inquiring into big existential questions. Opening up to the biggest and deepest context for human life that we can conceive of, expands our perception beyond the confines of our own subjective personal experience and creates fertile ground for out-of-the-box insights and liberating understandings. We might stumble upon all kinds of higher intuitions, illuminating visions and spiritual experiences in our life, but without a profound comprehension of the unhappy human condition in which we find ourselves, we will never be able to truly free ourselves from the predicament that is the source of our psychological suffering and our fundamental sense of limitation.

So let us begin this journey toward understanding this fundamental unhappy human condition by rewinding the tape to the beginning of our incarnated existence as a human being in this particular life in this realm called Earth. When we were born we appeared in this world without a clue as to our origins, having made no conscious choice to be here of which we were aware. The shock of being forcibly ejected from the all-encompassing warmth and preconscious contentment of our mother's womb into the jarring lights, shapes and sounds of this world was not an easy and effortless rite of passage. Our family members may have experienced our birth as a wondrous and happy occasion, but for us it was a traumatic event. Even though we did not have the self-awareness to consciously register that trauma at the time, we received it bodily, and the shock of it would only dissipate when we felt nurtured by the comfort and womb-like warmth of our mother's breast. Then, as we ceased our crying, we opened our eyes to gaze upon the scene before us. Radiating the pure, translucent light and fragrance of our undifferentiated consciousness and innocence, we bathed those who beheld us with our baby blessing. And we were bathed in return by the delight and adoration of our parents, and the other beings that beheld us.

As unselfconsciously happy and content as we were as babies much of the time, the psychic residue from the shock of our birth remained and we began to contract inwardly as we became primitively aware of our vulnerable state of bodily separateness. As we fed upon our mother's breast we were instinctually informed of this vulnerability and our separation from the preconscious contentment and sustenance that we experienced in our mother's womb.

This inevitable rite of passage from our undifferentiated consciousness as a baby into the early stages of individuation instigated our first experiences of fear, pain and abandonment. We began to experience a primal sense of deficiency or lack, the sense that we were hungry and therefore needed to be fed and protected. As we grew up this hunger was not only purely instinctual and physical, not only for the soothing ambrosia of our mother's milk and the warm glow of womb-like bodily comfort, it was an unconscious longing for the "paradise lost" of our previously undifferentiated state. This longing manifested as a craving for the gratification of all kinds of newly arising impulses that cascaded upon us as we began to interact with the spectrum of experience that life presented to us. During this period, often described in English as the "terrible twos", we were overwhelmed by impulsive emotional needs that demanded immediate fulfillment. And we all know what happens when the child does not or cannot get the immediate gratification it hungers for!

Of course that is not the whole story as we also evinced spontaneous delight and curiosity, as all children do in their unselfconscious innocence and playfulness. When we look into the eyes of babies and young children we see a disarmingly beautiful pure light, the light of the pre-personal being that looks out upon the world in wide open wonder, that simply sees but does not yet understand. That pure light of unselfconscious curiosity propelled us into the great adventure of life as we learned to walk, to talk, to feed ourselves, to communicate with others and so on. It was an exciting and challenging stage of trial and error, characterized by the innate drive to experience and to move forward. As soon as one challenge had been conquered we were ready for the next. From making sounds, to making words and learning how to read and write, from crawling to walking to being able to follow rules and participate in games, we experienced the warm glow of happiness and the delight of intimate interaction with our surroundings.

As we learned and individuated our consciousness became more polarized into a subject that confronted multiple objects. We became aware of our self as a distinct being facing an objective world that was sharing life in an expanded sphere of relations. This growing sense of psychophysical separateness was further intensified through our reactions to early experiences of emotional pain. Even if we were fortunate enough to grow up in a secure home with loving parents providing care, encouragement and the necessary means for our development, at some point we all learned that we could not ultimately depend on Mummy or Daddy for constant love, attention and sustenance. And so we began to feel anxious, unloved and even betrayed. We sulked, we complained, and we periodically broke out in uncontrollable tantrums as we began to dramatize the despair of the universal primal wound that afflicts all human beings – the wound of separation from our undifferentiated innocence.

The movement of seeking a remedy for this growing pain of isolation, unhappiness and abandonment was set in motion when we began to consciously make a connection between the acquisition of our desired object, person or activity, and the experience of relief from the pain of separate existence. Over time this pattern of seeking gradually conditioned us to project our energy and attention outward through our physical senses. Increasingly, when we looked out upon the field of phenomena that the world presented to us, we did not look with eyes of wide open wonder, but with the concentrating focus of our wanting and our deep need to be loved. This pattern of seeking from the outside what we instinctively felt to be lacking on the inside marked the beginning of the Great Search – the search for our sustenance, our fulfillment and our happiness in the realms of the body, mind and world.

By our teenage years our developing sexuality and the maturation of our physical body signaled the drive for independence from our parents. In our childhood we accepted the views and actions of our parents without question, but now we were developing the need to be the master of our own lives. We started wanting to do things our way and to have the freedom to do as we wished, but we also were not yet ready to be completely independent. Thus this was the real beginning of the development of our individual will. We wanted to be in control of our lives, we wanted to become self-determining and create a life that suited us. With this increasing need for independence and control, our sense of individuality went through a profound development accompanied by all the usual conflicts of adolescence that go with it.

Our mental faculty became sharper at this point; we developed the capacity to discriminate about what was desirable and what was possible for us. Needless to say, there was an intimate connection between our earlier adaptions and how our psychological development proceeded at this stage, because we were operating on the assumptions, beliefs and expectations that we picked up as children. Unlike physical development, which happens automatically, our psychological development requires that we actively participate in bringing it to full maturity. It requires that we learn to take responsibility for our own life, both inwardly and outwardly.

In tandem with this healthy process of individuation in adolescence came the not-so-healthy development, for most of us, of our narcissistic orientation towards life. Growing up in an intensely materialistic, individualistic modern culture with its endless smorgasbord of things to have and experiences to fulfill, we were increasingly captivated by the promise of the Great Search, by the exploitation of life for our own pleasure. And it is this almost hypnotic fascination with the promise of future fulfillment through the accumulation of experience and knowledge, that accompanied all of us into adulthood. This is why the Great Search is, to varying degrees, the driving tendency of the common or "worldly" adult who is rarely deeply happy or at ease with life as it is.

This is not to say that everything that we desire causes us to suffer. Free flowing, unselfconscious desire does not cause us suffering; for that is the movement of the pure force of Life. It is the force of Creation and Love Itself that animates our individual self-expression and the display of the entire universe. What we could call a "pure" desire is a spontaneous movement that manifests as an impulse to grow, to learn, to give and to celebrate life. Pure desire is purposed toward making our experience of life more wonderful, more deep, more rich, more complete. Just as unselfconscious curiosity propelled us into learning how to walk and talk as a child, this pure force of Life organically attracts us to experience as an adult, that deepens our maturity and our free enjoyment of being human. This is why we may be spontaneously drawn toward looking for a fulfilling relationship, creating a family, thriving in a rewarding career, getting a good education, playing a musical instrument or traveling the world. Pure, expansive desire of this kind does not cause us to suffer, but makes us feel alive, open, creative and free. But when the pure force of desire is refracted through the prism of our self-serving needs and wants, when our desire is motivated by the impulse to escape, or avoid, or by attachment, then the free flow of Life is curtailed and crystallized, as it contracts around a presumed point of independent self-existence, that we experience as being "me".

*****

By reflecting upon our developmental journey through life we can see that our sense of self has obviously evolved in all kinds of healthy psychophysical ways as our functions have grown and matured. In babyhood and early childhood our Life force was mostly devoted to growing physically and we were driven by instinct. In later childhood we began to develop emotionally and to be driven by impulsive needs. And as we grew into adolescence and early adulthood, we developed our mental capacities and our sense of self-determining will. We can also see that in conjunction with this process of individuation, our sense of "I" gradually contracted from an undifferentiated "I" that had no separate identity, to a subjective point of independent self-awareness seemingly located inside a body and identified with a mind.

For most of us that point of "I" – the independently existing sense of self – is felt to be located inside our head behind our eyes some-where. This inward sense of "I", that has gradually crystallized as a result of our adaptation to the spectrum of influences, relations and life conditions over the course of our development, appears to direct the continuity of "my" life, and identifies itself as being a particular person with a particular history. And since the original trauma of our birth, all of the shocks and traumas both great and small that we have endured and absorbed from the unloving actions of others and from our growing awareness of a less than hospitable world, have all reinforced this unexamined sense of being a separate, independent "I".

This developmental perspective helps us to see that the tightening of this self-contraction – the sense of a separate "I" – is an unavoidable aspect of the individuation process that all human beings go through. This understanding helps us to see how the remarkable process of indi-viduation – that "creates" multitudes of unique human expressions – is embedded in a kind of universal template. We are all unique human beings that have been influenced and shaped by so many different bi-ological, psychological and cultural factors, some for better and some for worse, none of which are exactly the same in any given lifetime. And yet a progressive contracting of the self-sense also accompanies this universal template of maturing individuation. In other words, we individuate and become distinct and unique through this process and, at the same time, we also self-contract into the universal human predicament of presumed separate existence that is the root cause of our suffering.

This is why the first noble truth of Gautama Buddha's teaching is that "Life is Suffering", and it is also what is signified by the Old Testament Christian myth of Adam and Eve and "the Fall of Man". This understanding does not necessarily imply that our experience of human existence is therefore destined to be a bleak affair of unremitting misery, it simply points to the fact that there is no avoiding "the Fall" into the condition of separate existence if we are born into this world of mortal conditional existence.

Once we have deeply observed, understood, and begun to authentically transcend, the conditioned patterning of the Great Search then, as the Buddha also taught, we can discover the Way out of suffering. Or, in Christian terms, we discover the path to Salvation. And then, as we shall see, that perennial Way of Spiritual Awakening leads us to both the *conscious* re-discovery of our undifferentiated True Nature *and* the True Fulfillment of the process of our individuation.

# Chapter 3

# Crossroads

WHEN we get to the point where we can no longer bear to maintain and feed the illusion of a mediocre and basically unhappy life that is contributing to our individual and collective suffering and insanity, then we come upon a fundamental sense of disillusionment. We may begin to profoundly feel the emptiness in getting what we want, to the degree that even when we get what we think we want we may experience a subtle dissatisfaction. More poignantly, we may even experience the arising of desire as a kind of quiet agony, a nagging dis-ease that we long to be relieved of. When we acquire the object, relationship or activity that we think we need and want, we increasingly find that its promise is empty and our usual satisfaction is short-lived. The existential questions "so what?" or "now what?" or "what is the point of it all?" may increasingly arise in the midst of our temporary experience of satiation, and our growing disillusionment with the momentum of seeking.

Many of us penetrate into this existential crossroads of fundamental disillusionment at some point in our lives. It is often the catalyst for what is commonly known as the "mid-life crisis", and more and

more people in their twenties and thirties these days are recognizing
that what they have been told and sold by mainstream culture is not
fulfilling them. But unfortunately, because of Western culture's patho-
logical addiction to the perpetual fantasy of future fulfillment, such a
crisis is usually viewed in a negative light. If we are not captivated and
compelled by the promises of money, power, sex and romance, then we
and others may presume that there must be something "wrong" with
us. However, as alone and insecure as we might feel as this disillusionment begins to dawn, allowing ourselves to confront this root sense of
despair is a true and necessary response to the unhappy human condition in which we find ourselves. If we are willing to bear and feel
into this existential emptiness with an open and courageous heart, we
will eventually come upon a clear-eyed clarity and acknowledgement
of the hard truth of conditional existence, and of our own mortality.

We will begin to see clearly that we pursue every kind of pleasure,
consolation and distraction so that we can experience some temporary relief from our pain of basic discontent and that, in so doing, we
desensitize ourselves to the stark reality of the situation we are in.
That stark reality is that the ultimate Happiness, Peace, Freedom and
Fulfillment that we seek cannot be found in the any of the objects,
activities and relationships that conditional existence provides. Why?
Because every thing, relationship, activity and state of mind that can
be experienced by the body-mind complex in this world, no matter
how pleasurable, no matter how sublime, no matter how consistent, is
*impermanent*. Think about it, everything, gross or subtle, that arises

eventually ceases. Every thing that is born is destined to die. Nothing that we can acquire in this realm of conditional experience will last. We do not want to experience loss, sorrow and separation, we do not want to suffer – and yet all of these conditions are unavoidable. Only if we are ready and willing to let this sobering truth deeply penetrate through the persistent patterning of the Great Search will we finally hit the "rock-bottom" reckoning with the devastating truth – that the promise of finding True Happiness, True Peace, True Freedom and True Fulfillment *in this world* is quite simply a very persuasive and insidious illusion.

*****

The stark reality of our situation is that no matter how relatively happy we may manage to become through acquiring what we desire in life, everything changes and we are bound to die. When we have the courage to face into this stark truth of impermanence and the inevitability of our own death, then we will see that no matter how good our life could possibly get in the experiential realms of body, mind and world, we *are going to die* and we are going to *lose everything*. Everything that we have possessed, known, achieved and experienced, and everyone and everything that we love, will be stripped away from us with the death of our individual body-mind.

If we are utterly convinced that all that we are *is* this individual body-mind personality that was born at a particular time, then coming upon this fundamental disillusionment will cause us to "crash". We will become emotionally depressed or cynically hardened in the face of what we now perceive to be a futile existence. We will then attempt to cover up that unbearable despair with addictive pleasures of various kinds, even though those pleasures become gradually less pleasurable, so that we can continue to live out the routines of our conventional or known "script" in the world.

This reaction of recoil in the face of existential disillusionment could be called "negative" despair. This malaise is very common especially in the most "developed" Western countries in which alarming numbers of the population are increasingly addicted to various kinds of anti-depressants, intoxicants, and the endlessly distracting omnipresence of electronic media. Nihilistic despair, corrosive cynicism and chronic depression, are ironically most endemic in cultures in which the potential for the individual to fulfill his or her personal desires has reached its apex.

Because the orientation of Western consumer culture, which has by now colonized almost the entire known world, is built upon the endless fantasy of the future fulfillment of the individual body-mind, Death is the greatest taboo. Conventional religion tends to console those who still hold to traditional values, by inventing a spiritualized future after bodily death in which all the things most valued in life are somehow eternalized in Heaven. On the other hand, the godless modern zeitgeist of scientific materialism is driven by the conviction that the exponentially increasing rate of technological progress – in computing, Artificial Intelligence, robotics, nanotech and biological engineering, etc. – is leading to a paradigm-shift in our fundamental state of existence. And this shift will also include the ability to radically extend our lifespans, so that we will have infinitely more time on Earth to enjoy these new capacities. This is what Ray Kurzweil, Google's chief technology officer, has dubbed "The Singularity", positing that there is a very good chance that these developments are all going to come together all at once to catalyze a monumental "tipping point" that will herald the advent of a "brave new world" of human evolution by unimaginable orders of magnitude. If he is right, Kurzweil and his fellow trans-humanists believe that this will be the best news in human history.

But in the East they have always been more realistic about the inherent ephemeralness of conditional existence. Death is acknowledged and not hidden away. The first time I actually saw a dead body was in India when I was twenty-four years old. I was sitting by the burning Ghats in Varanasi on the banks of the Ganges, which is one of the most auspicious places for a Hindu to be cremated. I was completely mesmerized by the sight of one funeral procession after another, accompanied by drums and the blowing of conch shells, arriving on the scene with a corpse, garlanded in beautiful flowers, that would then be cremated on the open fire. It was extraordinary to witness how death was so celebrated and openly exposed in Indian culture as the smell of burning flesh wafted by on the breeze. There was a deep shock of recognition that here I was, a grown adult, who had never been confronted with the most fundamental fact of existence – that fact being that "my" existence will end in death.

Death is hidden away in Western culture for a very good reason, because death confronts us with the ultimate meaninglessness of the Great Search for Happiness and Fulfillment in the realm of conditioned existence. Death is the obliteration of the subjective source of all meaning – our separate personal "I". When we deeply, not just intellectually, recognize that the desires of this "I", that we identify with as this body-mind, are *never* going to be fulfilled, and indeed *can never* be fulfilled in any ultimate sense, then we may come upon a truly "positive" despair or disillusionment. Positive, because instead of causing us to contract in upon our separate selves in horror, we may find ourselves breathing a deep sigh of relief, as we open out into an intuitive knowing that transcends the bounds of our mortal embodiment. A magnetic stillness, a sense of coming to rest, a mysterious freedom from our previously unquestioned presumption that we are *only* a mortal body-mind forever destined to suffer in the cycles of seeking, may quietly begin to dawn.

*****

Navigating this crossroads of positive disillusionment often generates great upheaval and our life circumstances may change dramatically as a result. We may find ourselves ending a long-term relationship, marriage or job, or moving to another place, because we now see and feel ourselves to be trapped and stifled by those circumstances. Or, while there may be a lot of inner turmoil, the current pattern of our relationships and responsibilities in our day-to-day life may not be so outwardly impacted. But in either case, a subtle yet profoundly pervasive shift occurs in our orientation to Life as a whole.

The compulsive drive to seek for happiness and fulfillment in the conventional field of possibilities by constantly projecting our energy and attention outward begins to diminish. The flickering allure of consumer culture loses its power to entice us. We tire of social expectations to conform, to compete, to "make it", to look sexy, and to be somebody in this world. The narratives and values of traditional religion, scientific materialism and modern rationalism no longer satisfy us. Humility begins to soften us, as we let in the truth that despite being intelligent, apparently mature, sensitive, independent adults, we do not yet know who we really are or why we are here. We allow ourselves to *feel into* our existential bewilderment, and to make friends with the inherent insecurity of life, as so many of the narratives, values and self-images that we have absorbed from our parents, teachers and cultural background, begin to buckle and break.

As we cross the threshold into the fresh, new and unknown adventure of Awakening, it is very common to feel like an outsider, adrift in a world that no longer makes sense. We no longer "fit in" to the prevailing current of cultural norms, narratives and social expectations. Traversing this Crossroads is usually a very insecure and disconcerting rite of passage that may last for several months or even many years.

As we free ourselves from the consensus matrix of the Great Search, a still, sober aloneness begins to emerge within us, and often, along with that, comes the intermittent fear, and even terror, of losing everything that was once held so dear – our cozy relationships, shared values, and material comforts. For some the fear and disorientation of being swept out into uncharted waters is simply too much to bear, and so they find a way to compromise their spiritual longing by falling back into patterns of living and relating that are comfortable, safe and known. But if living a life of mediocrity is no longer an option for us, then we will feel a rising intuitive certainty in our hearts that there can be no turning back. We will feel the thrilling tug of a Presence beyond our comprehension that calls us forward no matter how insecure it may make us feel.

When the hard truth of positive disillusionment has taken root, and we feel spontaneously moved toward the principle of Freedom from the conditioned pattern of mortal existence, then the Awakening Process has irrevocably begun, and there can be no turning back.

# Chapter 4

# The Fly on the Window

ONCE we have awakened to the futility of mankind's Great Search and have intuitively recognized what Gautama Buddha meant when he declared the principle "Life is suffering" to be the foundation of his teaching, we consciously begin to turn away from the conflicted cycle of seeking for our fulfillment in material and psychological terms. We usually then begin to identify ourselves, on some level, as now being a "spiritual seeker". This initiates our entrance into what Spiritual Master Adi Da called the "second" Great Search, the "first" Great Search being the conventional search for happiness in the gross, material domain of conditional existence.

The second Great Search is the search for spiritual or "ultimate" Fulfillment, which is commonly referred to as Enlightenment in the Eastern spiritual traditions or Salvation in the Middle Eastern monotheistic religions that spread throughout the West. This second Great Search is usually conceived as a turning away from the material, vital and mortal world of "Earth" and "Life" toward an inward search for the metaphysical, subtle and spiritual world of "Heaven" or "Light".

When most spiritual seekers sit down to meditate, pray or enact any spiritual practice, they tend to start from a presumption of themselves as an unenlightened, limited and contracted ego "I" or "sinner", who is then going to attempt to invert and project the urge to spiritual or ultimate Liberation or Fulfillment toward the "higher" subtle potentials of "Heaven" and "Light", via various techniques and methodologies. In other words, instead of directing attention "downwards and outwards" toward the conventional objects of the first Great Search into the earthly, vital realm of Life, they are now directing attention "inwards and upwards" toward the heavenly realm of Light. Instead of seeking "worldly" experience they are now seeking "spiritual" experience, and to enter into some kind of "alternative" transcendental Reality beyond the realms of the body and mind.

This orientation is almost inevitable, and very understandable in the early and intermediate stages of the spiritual path, until a more mature understanding and orientation replaces it. However, this immature orientation tends to persist in many Western spiritual seekers because we are so culturally conditioned to be narcissistic consumers of experience.

Chogyam Trungpa, a controversial Tibetan Master who pioneered the seeding of the Buddha-Dharma in the West, called this typically Western disease "spiritual materialism" and wrote an excellent book about it called *Cutting Through Spiritual Materialism* that I highly recommend. If you want to get a sense of this in yourself it is a basic disposition in relationship to the spiritual path that seeks relief and consolation in accumulating psychic or mystical experience, and also seeks to develop a self-consciously "spiritual" identity. If your orientation to spirituality consists of desires like the following: "I want to feel better, to feel peaceful and blissful all the time", "I want to escape from the complexity of bodily, emotional and mental life", and if you find yourself attracted to adorning your body or abode with spiritual paraphernalia – then this indicates that your longing for liberation carries the taint of spiritual materialism.

*****

Once we have embarked upon the second Great Search in earnest, instead of seeking Happiness, Fulfillment and Freedom through the acquisition of objects, relationships and activities, we now seek Happiness, Fulfillment and Freedom through the acquisition of higher states of consciousness. And, especially in the post-modern, "alternative", East-meets-West spiritual marketplace, there is now a veritable smorgasbord of spiritual methodologies and technologies available, that if pursued will indeed generate often remarkable and deeply liberating higher states of consciousness. Assuming that we have enough passion and persistence (and are willing to spend the money), it is not so difficult these days to experience higher or extraordinary states of consciousness by practicing yoga, pranayama, rebirthing, shamanism, tantra and mantras, etc. However, whatever goes "up" has to come "down" and "Heaven" cannot be taken by storm. Higher states, or what are often called "peak" experiences, can indeed give us a "peek" or glimpse of what is possible, but all experiential states must, by definition, eventually fade because, as I mentioned before, all experiences including states of consciousness, are *impermanent*. This is why so many spiritual seekers *remain* spiritual *seekers* for their entire lives. Addicted to the fleeting ecstatic highs and incandescent lights of subtle and mystical experience, they are perpetually in the grip of the patterning of the second Great Search that seeks to *acquire* spiritual Enlightenment or Salvation. Thus they are constantly compelled to keep seeking for the ever-elusive magical "Enlightenment bullet" that they think is going to propel them into a never-ending experience of Bliss and Love and Light.

However, as embedded as our tendency to be consumers is in our Western psyches, if we are sincere in our aspiration for Awakening, and sensitive to the positive disillusionment that underlies *all* seeking, at some point we will recognize that the ultimate Happiness, Peace, Freedom and Fulfillment we seek can only be discovered by *letting go of seeking completely.*

*****

An amusing metaphor that often comes to mind to explain this is that of a fly desperately buzzing and banging its head over and over again on the window through which it sees the Light. It excitedly traverses the window by buzzing upwards, downwards, sideways, in every possible direction. It rests for a while and starts again, always finding itself frustrated by the beckoning of the Light that seems closer than close, yet forever out of reach. At some point, completely exhausted from its ferocious buzzing and its repeatedly bashing its head against the glass, it finally gives up trying to penetrate through the window to the Light beyond, and is then spontaneously overtaken by a mysterious "out-of-the-box" impulse. Letting go of the tension of *seeking* the Light, it relaxes its linear approach and then unexpectedly discovers an open window or door nearby and buzzes effortlessly out into the Light of Freedom.

In this metaphor the window obviously represents the seeking mind, through which Enlightenment or Awakening is usually pursued, and the open window or door represents the possibility of Freedom that is *always already* the case, but can only be apprehended when we let go of all seeking. All the true spiritual teachings and teachers tell us that True Happiness, Peace, Freedom and Fulfillment are closer than close, right in front of our noses, and yet we cannot get "there" from "here". As long as we *presume* that our separation from the Light is already the case, or "here", then we will be forever banging our head on the window trying to get "there". When we finally give up and let go of all seeking, after having exhausted all our efforts and strategies, in that still, silent dawning, however it occurs, we become sensitized to a deep intuition of innate Happiness, Peace and Freedom that is not dependent on the attainment of any object or experience. This intuition tells us that our natural state is *already* Happy, Free and at Peace, and that whatever is natural to us must be with us *always*.

# Part II

# IGNITION OF THE HEART

# Chapter 5

# The Fire of the Heart

IF YOU resonate with the longing for True Happiness, Peace, Freedom and Fulfillment, and also with the sense of positive disillusionment with the conditioned cycles of seeking that I have described, then you are ripe and ready to ignite and step into the Fire of the Heart.

By Heart with a capital H, I mean the Spiritual Heart, not the physical heart. That Heart is synonymous with signifiers for our True Nature such as "Consciousness", "Spirit" or "God", which I will use liberally throughout this book.

So what do I mean by the Fire of the Heart? The Fire of the Heart is a longing that *burns*. Unlike any other desire it is a longing that is not focused on or satisfied by the material objects, relationships and activities that the world has to offer. There is something mysterious about it, something indefinable, something infinitely captivating and magnetic. It is not so much a longing *for* something in particular, but is rather a longing for Liberation *from* all that binds and limits us. In essence, it is a longing to discover, realize and release *Who We Really Are*.

This longing might be experienced at times as a very still, quiet, whispering tug of intuitive knowing, or at other times, as an intense burning urge for radical transformation, or anything in between. However it makes itself known, this Fire of the Heart streams up from the core of our being spontaneously. It is a longing for growth, for self-transcendence and for the full flowering of our humanity. It is a longing to break free of psychological and cultural conditionings that keep us bound to repeating patterns of thought, emotion and action. It is a longing to venture into new and undiscovered realms of free energy and free creativity. It is a longing to Awaken into a wider, deeper and infinitely more passionate and ecstatic life. No thing or particular experience that the world can offer us can quench this longing. Only one thing will suffice: the on-going Revelation and ever-growing Realization of the inherent Truth, Love and Goodness that is the essence of our Being and of Life itself.

*****

When we make ourselves available to the Fire of the Heart, we find ourselves in a paradoxical state in which one-pointed intent and wide-open receptivity merge and become one. When we give ourselves wholeheartedly to the Fire of the Heart we discover that our one-pointed intention to Free ourselves from identification with binding biological, psychological and cultural patterns, and our open receptivity to a Mystery that transcends all knowing, become one unified disposition.

Intention is the active force of will that issues from our limited finite sense of self and figuratively reaches up to "knock on the door" of Heaven or the transpersonal dimensions of Being. And surrender is the gesture of yielding, the emptying of self, which opens the vehicle of our body-mind to draw down and receive the infusion of Conscious Light or, in Christian terms, the inpouring of the Holy Spirit.

Intention is the more agented, more penetrative, and we could say more masculine, aspect of asserting ourselves, of putting ourselves in God's way, so to speak. Intention implies determination, courage, persistence, and an inner disposition that boldly declares "I want to be Free". Surrender is the more receptive, yielding, and we could say more feminine, pole of this paradoxical alchemy. Surrender implies devotion to a Mystery that the mind can never understand, a willingness to not know and to trust that our True Nature is *already* Free. Both qualities need to be activated in the individual man or woman, and to fuse as one posture, one gesture, and one disposition in and as the Heart. It is this inner posture of intention and surrender that ignites and fuels the enlightening and purifying trajectory of the Awakening Process.

As you listen for and give yourself to the call of the Fire of the Heart you will find that you become sensitized to the artful integration of both of these qualities. At one moment you may need to lean toward one pole or the other in navigating your way through the demands and challenges of life. At times you will need to push, to make effort, and at other times you need to yield, to let go. As this intuitive capacity deepens, and becomes more and more consistent in your experience, you will be increasingly capable of transcending the conditioned patterning of separated, limited and conflicted existence that stifles your radiant Spirit.

All authentic approaches to spiritual life imply and require the practice of discipline. Spiritual practice or discipline is the mechanism of self-transcendence. While there are many different approaches, techniques and methodologies that have been described and elaborated by all the spiritual traditions, the greatest and most effective discipline on any spiritual path is to simply surrender to the Fire of the Heart. Simply acknowledge and accept that this flame *is* alive within you. If you undeniably feel that it is alive within you then the potential for your own Awakening and Transformation is undeniably real.

If the discovery and realization of spiritual Freedom, Happiness, Peace and Fulfillment are of paramount importance, if you are ready to let go of any expectation or demand about what the Awakening Process is and how it should happen, then the bud of Awakening is ready to flower. If you truly allow the Fire of the Heart to overwhelm you in this way, then you will begin to intuit the presence of an immeasurable, uncontainable Mystery that is both who you essentially are, and is simultaneously much vaster than anything you ever imagined as being "you".

*****

This profound offering and consecration of our Being to the Fire of the Heart is the most essential ingredient on any authentic spiritual journey. Why is this intensity of aspiration so essential? Because otherwise, when we are confronted with all the forces, within and without, that resist and revolt against the Awakening Process, we will inevitably falter, doubt and eventually turn away to find consolation in some illusion, in some mode of life in which we will settle for less than the complete fruition and fulfillment of our precious human birth.

It is our commitment to Awakening that will carry us through all the trials and challenges that the journey from unconsciousness to Consciousness brings. We all commit ourselves to something in each and every moment of our lives. In every moment we are either moving toward or away from our deepest understanding and intuition of what is most True, Good or Beautiful. So if we seriously want to Awaken, if we sincerely want to transform, our passion for and surrender to the Fire of the Heart must be stronger than any other desire.

Many who undertake a spiritual path may do all kinds of practices, attend retreats and workshops, and may be involved in various "good works", all of which may be genuine, valuable and may result in positive benefits for themselves and others, but without the essential ingredient of this profound surrender to the Fire of the Heart these activities and experiences will not result in a deep and consistent transformation.

While it takes a measure of commitment to give oneself to a regular meditation practice for example, the aspiration I am speaking about has no limits, transcends all forms, and can be present in all activity. This longing for Liberation, this Fire of the Heart, if it is profound, is not something that we can fit into our pre-existing lives. This heartfelt aspiration is a constant attunement, a living assertion of and alignment with Truth, with Life, with Love that is constantly being affirmed and reaffirmed at the core of our Being. We will know that this flame is irrevocably alive in us when we no longer need to remember it, when we cannot forget it, and when it becomes the very animating force and guiding principle of our life.

I cannot emphasize enough how absolutely essential this passionate aspiration for Awakening is. All that happens arises from the commitment that you and I make in this very moment. When we are truly willing to give everything to that longing NOW then a shift occurs at the core of our Being that makes all things possible. Then that longing will define every important choice that we make in our life, and will surely carry us Home.

# Chapter 6

# I AM

THE WISDOM traditions that have come to us from the East tell us that our unhappiness, discontent, and misery are not primarily caused by events or circumstances, but by our ignorance of who or what we really *are*. As long as we limit ourselves by identifying solely with an individual body-mind as who we are, then we will feel desire for whatever we think is needed for the survival and fulfillment of this body-mind, and we will fear and dislike whatever threatens its survival or comfort. When we do not get whatever we desire or like, and when we cannot avoid what we fear or dislike, then we suffer and feel unhappy and discontented. Therefore, when we are suffering as result of our ever fluctuating likes and dislikes, desires and fears, we can potentially understand that we are lost in ignorance and lacking in clear knowledge of our True Nature.

But if we are lost in ignorance, as these time-honoured teachings tell us, what is it that we are ignoring? If we are lost in the ever-changing currents of our desires and fears, and the ever-changing world of objects, relationships and activities, how do we discover that which is unchanging or eternal?

What we are ignoring is the radical simplicity of who we really *are* prior to the arising of the body, mind and world. And it is through releasing our attention from the phasing cycles of desire and fear that we can begin to discover this eternal dimension of our Being.

As I have already explained, this Being is not an experience or state to be attained through seeking, it is the primary and most direct experience that we are *always already* having. But we tend to overlook it because we are habitually always projecting our attention and energy *outwards*, away from our most fundamental state of Being.

*****

Our essential Being is an open secret staring us in the face. It is closer than close and is actually impossible to avoid. Let me prove it to you in your own direct experience right *now...*

You know that you exist. Only because you exist can you know the existence of other things. You know your own Being because you are conscious. Without Consciousness your Being would not be known and without Being Consciousness could not exist. Thus your Being and your Consciousness of Being are inseparable. In fact they are identical and both are expressed in the single phrase "I am". I AM THAT I AM is what God is said to have declared to Moses as told in the Old Testament, and indeed your Consciousness of I AM is prior to all experience, and is the source and foundation of all knowledge.

This essential Being-Consciousness that you *are* is the same Being-Consciousness that I essentially *am* and everyone and every sentient being essentially *is*. Yet our knowledge of this Being-Consciousness of

I AM is confused. We believe that "I am...this body, I am...this person, I am...fifty years old, I am...sad or happy, I am...a good person, a bad person, an ugly or beautiful person, I am...British or Portuguese or German or American, I am this, and I am that, and I am definitely not this or that", and on it goes from the moment we wake up in the morning to last thing at night.

Then, when we dream at night, we take on a dream body and are convinced that we are that dream character in an equally convincing dream world until we wake up and say, "Ah it was only a dream." At this point we consciously recognize that we were not the one in the dream. When we relinquish the states of both waking and dreaming we dissolve into deep sleep and every notion of being a body-mind in a world completely disappears. Yet *we* don't disappear. "I AM" obviously still remains otherwise we could not say, "I slept well" in the morning. By reflecting on our actual experience of the three states of waking, dreaming and deep sleep, it becomes clear that our experience of being a body-mind character in a "waking" world or even a "dream" world is not continuous. The only aspect of our experience that is continuous is I AM. In Hindu Vedanta they call this I AM Presence "Turiya", which means the ever-present "fourth state" which transcends and includes the three states of waking, dreaming and deep sleep.

That which mistakes the body to be "I" is the mind. Our mind comes into existence only upon imagining that it is a body. As soon as we wake up from dream or deep sleep the mind arises along with the

sense that "I am" so and so, I am this body. Only after identifying itself as a particular body, does the "I" perceive the apparently external
world through the five senses of the body. Interestingly, exactly the
same thing happens in a dream. When the "I" identifies itself with a
dream body it perceives the apparently external dream world through
the senses of its dream body. When we wake up from the dream we
understand that the body we mistook to be "I", and the world we
mistook to be real, were both in fact ultimately unreal creations of
our Consciousness. Knowing that our Consciousness has this incredible power of creation, is it not reasonable to suspect that the body we
take to be "I", and the world we take to be real in our present waking
state may in fact be nothing more than a mere projection of our Consciousness, just like the world and body we experience in a dream?
What evidence do we have that our body in this waking state, and
the world we perceive through the senses of this body, are anything
other than a creation of Consciousness? There is no way we can prove
to ourselves that the world exists independent of our perception of it,
because any proof that we may wish to rely upon can come only from
the world whose reality we are questioning.

Therefore, if we want to discover the answer to such a captivating
existential question, we have to find a way to go beyond the three
states of waking, dreaming and deep sleep. So how do we Awaken
from the waking dream of the separate personal "I" to the ever-present
"fourth state"? How do we free ourselves from such an embedded and
persistent illusion? We can study spiritual books and scriptures and

gain an intellectual understanding of our True Nature, but it is only authentic direct experience and insight that can truly liberate and grace us with the discovery of the True Happiness, Peace, Freedom and Fulfillment that is *always already* the case.

In this book I will endeavor to evoke, provoke and facilitate that Direct Awakening to your True Nature, primarily through what I am calling True Meditation. But before I "zoom in" to explore that Direct Awakening, I am first going to "zoom out" once again so that we can better understand the nature of the separate ego "I" that is the mechanism of our embedded and tenacious ignorance.

# Chapter 7

# E-G-O

THE CONDITION of ignorance of our True Nature is commonly referred to as the false self or "ego" in spiritual teachings. The term "ego" in a spiritual context refers to the separate, personal "I" that identifies itself solely with the individuated body-mind and its historical story. It is important to understand that the term "ego" when used in a spiritual context is different from the definition that is often utilized in Western psychology, which usually refers to the self-organizing, integrating or unifying principle in the psyche. That "functional ego" or individuated self-sense is a very necessary adaption of the whole being that needs to be in good working order for us to act and navigate in the world. In fact if this "self-organizing principle" is not yet stable in an individual then they tend to exhibit forms of extreme neurosis and erratic behaviour, which makes entering into an authentic spiritual path inadvisable and even dangerous.

It is sometimes said that we have to develop a "healthy" ego before we can realistically and authentically engage in the process of transcending it. There is much truth to this in that we must reach a point in our development in which we can demonstrate an integrated responsibility for the whole living being, physical, emotional and mental. This means that our individual self-expression is fundamentally stable and that we have the capacity to be present throughout both the frustrating and pleasurable conditions of born existence. Some of the important qualities of mature adulthood include a more or less consistent emotional stability, appropriate discipline, open mindedness, self-reliance, patience, a realistic self concept and a capacity for discernment and commonsense. The fact that many adults fail to arrive at this point of a healthy integrated self is demonstrated in the prevalence of social problems such as alcoholism, drug addiction, violence, racism, depression and various forms of neurosis.

*****

While it is important to be clear that the term "ego" in a spiritual context does not refer to the self-organizing principle in the psyche, it is also important to understand that it does not refer to our personality either. Our personality, which has been shaped by all kinds of factors both known and unknown, is the unique "sheath" or outer layer of our individual self-expression. Indeed, "persona" is the Latin word for "mask", and if we break the meaning of the word down further, we find that "pers" means "through" and "sona" means "to be heard". So our personality is the "mask" or sheath through which we are heard and expressed in the world. Now of course most people presume that they *are* their personality, but if we understand that our personality is simply a "mask" or sheath through which we express ourselves then, if we are aligned with a deeper trans-personal dimension of our Being, our personality or "mask" will potentially be a unique sheath through which that greater Being expresses itself. So Awakening to who we really are *beyond* the persona or "mask" does not neutralize our unique personality, rather it *liberates* our personality; it animates and brightens it with the Light of the True Self. As we shall see and understand more profoundly as we explore the nature of the Awakening Process throughout this book, it is our attachment to needing to be someone who is *separate and special* in his or her uniqueness that distorts the natural and free expression of our personality.

*****

So if the ego "I" is not the self-organizing principle in the psyche and if it is not our unique personality, then what is it exactly? It might appear that the ego must be something very vague and elusive. However, it is not vague and elusive at all once we know where to look. Simply put, it is a habitual and usually unconscious *contraction* of our experience of being conscious. It is a self-generated diminishment of the fundamental Happiness, Peace, Freedom and Fullness of Existence. When we simply abide in the essential experience of I AM prior to identification with body, mind and world, prior to any interpretation whatsoever, there is no fundamental sense of separateness or unhappiness or stress. Everything simply IS and we simply ARE. We will dive into a profound exploration of this radical simplicity of our True Nature as we proceed, but if all of this is new to you just getting an intuitive sense of it for now will suffice.

Think of the times when you were or are the happiest, the most spontaneous, the most joyful and creative, when you experience the most effortless communion with those around you and your surroundings. Are those not the times when you forget yourself, when you are free from self-consciousness, when you, for whatever reason, drop your personal story? When we free our energy and attention from exclusive self-identification with body, mind and personal history, there is no division or differentiation occurring in the field of our experience. Only then do we potentially glimpse the truth that our very familiar sense of being a "skin encapsulated" personal, separate "I" is created by a chronic psychosomatic contraction that keeps our native Happiness, Peace, Freedom and Fulfillment more or less constantly at bay. And in the instant of our identification with this presumed sense of separateness everything else that arises in the field of our awareness is presumed to be other than "me" and therefore "out there".

*****

If you look closely into your own experience you will recognize that at the core of this self-contraction is an embedded sense of deficiency, of lack, a sense that something is wrong, something is missing. Think of the innocence with which you gazed upon the world when you were a young child, and then the gradual tensing of your energy and attention into the concentrated focus of your developing self-identity and its fears and desires as you grew up. It is that tensing or tightening that creates the *powerful illusion of independent self-existence – the sense of a separate I that I call "me"*.

It is this conditioned reflex of separateness that causes us to suffer unnecessarily. It is not the experience of being an individual with a body and mind expressing a personality that causes us to suffer psychologically. What causes us to suffer is our unexamined attachment to this deeply conditioned reflex that identifies our experience of individuality as being a separate island of self-consciousness "in here", that stands independent from all "others" and all of manifest reality "out there".

A simple way to define this contraction of consciousness is to say that EGO – E-G-O – means Edging God Out! The ego "I" that is exclusively confined to the separate psychophysical island of our self-identity effectively pushes (or "edges") everything else out of the sphere of its concern.

*****

The grosser manifestations of ego consciousness are relatively easy to recognize in our own experience and in our observation of others. Simply put, ego is the "I" that feels habitually alienated and unhappy. It is the "I" that always has a problem to overcome, the "I" that is convinced that there is "something wrong", the "I" that is chronically victimized by the shifting circumstances of life. Ego is the "I" that clings to security and desperately needs to be loved and affirmed. It is the "I" that feels compelled to dominate, to prove, to be right and to win an argument. It is the "I" that is chronically double-minded, that is always saying "Yes" and "No" – either "Yes" and "No" simultaneously or else sometimes "Yes" and sometimes "No". The ego "I" always keeps its options open and so can never become one-pointed or straightforward about anything.

Ego is the "I" that is so narcissistically self-focused that it is devoid of genuine spontaneity, compassion and love. The ego "I" refers every experience back to itself and is therefore self-centered by definition. Always turned in upon itself, thinking about itself, worrying about itself, the ego "I" is always checking inwardly, as people and events present themselves, "What's in it for *me*?"

The more self-centered we are the more conflict even small problems create in our mind. The stronger our sense of being a separate ego, the narrower the scope of our thinking becomes; then even small situations can become unbearable. On the other hand, if we concern ourselves mainly with others, if we open to the totality of life, if we take our attention off of our "problems", then the broader our sphere of concern becomes and life's inevitable difficulties disturb us less.

When we are identified with ego-based emotions we tend to be in either a stimulated, excited and restless state activated by *desiring* – hence rage, jealousy, greed and lust – or in a depressed, passive or inert state activated by *fear* – hence inertia, envy, shame and victimization. Emotion literally means "disturbance" from the Latin word "emovere", which means, "to disturb". The emotional weight of the ego is usually due to past emotional associations being unconsciously projected onto the present moment and circumstance. Hence, the actuality of *what is* in the present moment is disturbed or clouded by the overlay of emotion. Hence one of the most common and easily recognizable ego-based emotions is resentment, which literally means to "feel again".

Ego-based emotions that are generated by selfish desire are generally easy to locate in our experience. Driven by the need to have and to possess, the seeking energies of attachment, jealousy, greed and lust are obvious examples. In mentioning lust I do not mean to suggest that the arising of sexual desire is ego-based, but to indicate what happens when it is filtered through our own selfish wanting. The natural biological impulse of sex is then constricted and one sees the other as a sexual object for the potential release of the tension of that desire.

When life confronts us with challenges that demand change on some level we usually feel fear, and then often contract by identifying with the life numbing pull into inertia, into stasis and depression. In this state we easily feel victimized by other people and outer circumstances, and feel drained of all creative power. A common emotion that paralyses our ability to respond freely to life is shame, and its closely associated emotion of guilt. The healthy side to these emotions has to do with conscience and remorse, which is activated when we allow ourselves to empathize and to feel the impact of actions that cause pain and suffering to others. If our relationship to shame and guilt is healthy, then we will receive them as important sources of information that enable us to take responsibility for those actions. We may do that through an apology for example, and then we can let go of the shame or guilt. However, if we are more concerned with how our "negative" actions reflect on our own self-image, more than we are on the impacts of our actions on others, then we will tend to dwell on the emotions of shame and guilt. We may even get some morbid pleasure out of beating ourselves up and feeling unworthy. Shame also manifests as the painful sense of being exposed as defective, whether by others or by our own "inner critic". The voice of our inner critic is usually a composite of the shaming voices we were subjected to as children that we then turn upon ourselves in adulthood. By identifying with and giving power to the voice of the inner critic and its associated emotion of shame, we create and reinforce a negative self-image. Because shame is a sensation of frustrated self-protection rooted in fear, it can quickly mutate into cold-hearted withdrawal or passive aggression.

Probably the most important thing we need to be on the look out for if we want to observe, understand, and ultimately transcend the mechanism of ego, is pride. Pride indicates the assumption and position that "I already know". Pride is the basic defense mechanism of the self-contraction of ego. Pride is the emotional and mental investment in being right, in being separate, and in being special in some form. Thus it is pride that creates the hard shell of ego. We can most easily recognize it in others and ourselves as a hardness of heart. It is the wall that rises up when we perceive that we are being attacked, when our self-image is being threatened, when something is being revealed about us that we do not want to face.

Pride creates a very strong wall of rigid resistance to any information that would challenge the edifice of the self-contraction of the ego. When challenged pride can very easily and quickly turn vicious and magnify its expression through anger and violence. But pride does not only manifest in the most obvious forms of arrogance and superiority, pride can also manifest as victimization, shame and inferiority, because at the core of these emotions there is still the strong investment in a position of separateness and specialness.

Pride also manifests as our attachment to certain beliefs, concepts and opinions. If we get angry when someone challenges a particular belief or opinion that we hold dear, whether it pertains to ourselves, to a particular area of knowledge or to an event in the external world, it is a clear indication that we are attached to that idea, and we are not open to questioning it. We tend to build our self-identity around certain strong beliefs and what we think that we know. In my own experience I have observed that pride and the "need to know" are the primary obstacles to the self-transcending process for most intelligent and sensitive men, because men tend to be deeply conditioned to gain security through knowing, and as a result identify strongly with their accumulated knowledge.

Pride can also be extremely subtle and disguise itself in notions of specialness that are imperceptible to us. Pride will almost definitely join us on our journey of Awakening in some shape or form. Therefore, we always need to be vigilant and on the lookout for subtle movements of superiority and self-satisfied identification with spiritual knowledge and experience as we engage in the Awakening process. The further we go the more we will be attracted to the open-ended emptiness and freedom of being nobody, rather than the need to be somebody. However, we can never underestimate the subtle and tenacious movements of ego that can undermine and corrupt the purity of our motive every step of the way.

Pride is also at the root of cynicism, another expression of ego that is very common in our times. Cynicism is a particularly postmodern disease, a corrosive posture in relationship to life that says, "I already know that it is not possible". What is not possible? Goodness, Truth, Beauty, Love, Innocence. Close cousins of cynicism are irony and endemic pessimism and fatalism. These are all postures of an often very clever and sophisticated ego that evinces a disdain for any kind of innocent, hopeful, unselfconscious passion for life. The nimble and witty banter of irony and cynicism is often amusing and titillating, but underneath it there often lurks a biting superiority and disenchantment with life that insidiously erodes our Spiritual Heart. If we truly aspire to be Free, Happy and deeply Fulfilled human beings, then all the cynicism has to go.

Underneath all forms of pride, which as I said earlier is the primary defense mechanism of ego, lies the sensation that is at the core of our self-contraction, which is fear. We fear not knowing, we fear being exposed and we fear being nobody. All of the fears of the ego "I" issue from our core fear of dissolution and death, the primal fear that our habitual activity of identifying with the self-contraction of separateness will be revealed for the illusion that it really is.

When circumstances conspire to confront and challenge us to face and let go of our pride, and the fear that lies beneath it, then doubt often raises its head. Indeed, one way that we can define fear is that it is a *temptation* to doubt. Doubt is like a wily snake whispering in our ear. If we are not very careful the voice of doubt can deviously colonize our mind and insidiously co-opt our rational capacities to undermine the Awakening Process. The ego, in the guise of doubt, makes a virtue out of asserting its independence from the perceived spiritual slavery to a higher selfless motivation for being alive. It will gather whatever evidence it can to support its counterfeit authority, and it will righteously rewrite history to bolster its destructive agenda. So we have to be very careful when doubt raises its head, because if we identify with it we can easily and rapidly undermine our own spiritual progress and confidence and, in so doing, hinder our direct access to the wellsprings of Innocence, Goodness, Truth and Beauty.

*****

At the core of our developmental trajectory from babyhood to childhood to adolescence to adulthood is the progressive crystalliza-tion of the separate psychophysical "I". Like a snowball rolling down a snowy mountain this self-contraction gathers momentum, and by the time we reach mature adulthood, it has usually Edged-God-Out (E-G-O) to such a degree that an almost continuous sense of psychological isolation, gnawing lack, and restless seeking is presumed to be quite "normal", even "natural" and "only human". But once we begin to authentically Awaken, we intuit that this condition, as convincing as it may appear to be most of the time, is actually "abnormal", "unnat-ural" and perhaps even "sub-human". We might even recognize that this "human condition", as it is popularly conceived of at this point in our evolution as a species, is in a dangerously diseased and deluded condition bordering on collective insanity. If my words appear extreme than simply consider the fact that in the 21$^{st}$ century the human race is in very grave danger of driving itself to the brink of extinction and is destroying its own Mother, our precious and beautiful blue green Earth, at an evermore alarming rate.

Why is the self-contraction of the ego "I" so destructive? Because it is the activity in all of us that sees, and feels itself to be separate from the other, and from all of Life. This sense of being an isolated separate ego shuts us off from the living truth of our *absolute interrelatedness* with everything that is. As long as we remain addicted to the selfish agenda of the unhappy ego "I" and its Great Search, then we are only contributing to the state of dangerously arrested development that is afflicting humanity as a whole. Seen in that light the rapidly converging crises – ecological, social and economic – of our time are, for those of us who have the eyes to see and the ears to hear, a systemic spiritual call to Awaken and to Evolve. And not just for our own sake, but for the sake of humanity, for the sake of our shared Earth, and for the sake of the further Evolution of Life itself.

That may seem like a daunting task (and it is!), but as you will discover if you take to Heart what I am going to share with you from this point forward, the ego "I" is not truly you or I, or anyone else and never has been. For in truth who you *really* are, who we *all* really are, is *not* a fixed, static, wounded, deficient, unhappy entity that goes by a particular name and is defined by a particular personal history. As we will discover, the apparent solidity and continuity of the ego "I" is nothing more than a deeply conditioned *activity* of identification with a complex web of psychological and cultural patterns. In essence, the ego "I" is nothing more than a case of *mistaken identity*.

The good news of Spiritual Awakening is that the habitual human "operating system" of separation, lack, and seeking, is not something that is happening to you. It is not a hardwired psychophysical program that you are helplessly at the mercy of, because it is in fact *your own action*. This is the key insight, the liberating "hard" truth that unlocks the door to the Awakening Process. As Spiritual Master Adi Da used to say, when you realize that your suffering is due to the fact that you are pinching yourself, you simply stop pinching!

As long as we persist in the activity of habitual identification with the conditioned web of psychological and cultural patterns we will continue to experience ourselves as a separate, limited, historically defined, skin encapsulated "body mind" entity, living in the midst of other "body mind" entities, who are all incessantly seeking release from the pain of their own self-contracted existence. That Great Search – the conventional search for Fulfillment, Happiness and Love – is the perpetual dramatization of desire. It is the endless seeking of the ego "I" for union with various forms of experience that promise fulfillment but that, like everything else in this world, will all inevitably change and die in the end.

# Chapter 8

# The Whirlpool
# and the Ocean

As THE intuition of Awakening begins to dawn, we see and feel that the ego "I" is by its nature a contraction of being that is ignorant of its inherence in a far Greater Being. Imagine a whirlpool appearing in the ocean sucking water into itself. Then imagine that the whirlpool presumes itself to be a "something" that is other than the ocean, other than water. The powerful illusion that the ego "I" creates is exactly like that. It is a psychophysical whirl, or repeating pattern in consciousness, that presumes itself to be other than and independent of the wider ocean of Consciousness in which it appears. That is why when we try to look for the ego "I" we cannot actually locate it. All we can find is water, or Consciousness!

So what creates the illusion that the whirlpool is other than the ocean? What is it that creates the contracted experience of the inner, separate "I" and keeps it continuously turning in upon itself?

The spiritual traditions such as Buddhism and Vedanta that come to us from the East, tell us that this predicament is due to primordial ignorance. It is our ignoring of, or turning away from, the ocean of Being that always already sustains and transcends our individuality. Thus our ignorance, or our "fall" into born existence, is a *forgetting* of our Prior Unity with the ocean, with All That Is. And that forgetting makes it appear as if our sense of self – the whirlpool in this metaphor – is separate from the wider ocean of Being in which it arises.

The "Good News" of the genuine Enlightenment teachings is that the ego is not some kind of sub-personality or sinful demonic entity living inside of us. It is a present, deeply habitual *activity* of exclusive self-identification with our psychophysical experience that expresses itself symptomatically as every kind of constriction and limitation we experience. It is the self-contraction of the ego "I" that numbs, deadens and alienates us from the wellsprings of Love, Goodness and Truth that are the hallmarks of a liberated humanity.

The self-bound or self-contracted ego is always under stress. And this stress is always generating physical discomfort, boredom and all kinds of emotional reactivity and doubt. Therefore, the self-contracted and dependent individual is always seeking all kinds of knowledge and experience in order to find distraction and release from boredom, doubt, and discomfort. But there is no freedom from self-bound stress unless the self-contraction, with all of its dependency on objects, activities and relationships, is deeply understood and transcended. Then our native Happiness, Peace, Freedom and Fulfillment shines forth unimpeded and unveiled. It is the self-contraction of the ego "I" that *is* the presumption of unhappiness, of lack, of deficiency, that I mentioned at the beginning of the first chapter. And it is that presumption that *is* the seed of the seeking urge toward objects.

Therefore, to Awaken and authentically transform we must break free of our identification with the whirlpool of the self-contracted ego "I". Only then can our sense of individuality be founded on Truth, only then can we expand and merge into an oceanic Awakened "I" – that transcends the psychophysical dimensions of body, sensation, emotion and mind. Then, in proportion to the degree that we can deliver ourselves from the self-contraction of the ego, we will command a greater Happiness, a more profound wisdom, and a wider and infinitely more creative life.

If some recognition of what I have described above is dawning within you, or has already dawned within you, then you are that uncommon man or woman who stands at the door to Liberation. Having seen the intrinsic falsity and absurdity of the ego's game, you have now harnessed the fundamental understanding and power needed to deconstruct its dominion over your experience of individuated embodiment. And in so doing, you will reclaim your energy and attention for the great task of self-understanding and self-transcendence, so that you may be released into the Great Adventure of an authentically Awakened Life.

# Part III

# TRUE MEDITATION

# Chapter 9

# Beyond Mindfulness

$S$INCE the 1960's and 70's many spiritual teachings and practices have come to us from the East and, as a result, meditation along with yoga, has become increasingly popular in the progressive East-meets-West "alternative" culture. This cross-pollination has accelerated further in the 21st century as meditation is now gaining greater popularity and application in mainstream society, mostly under the moniker of "Mindfulness". The Mindfulness movement largely teaches practices originally derived from Buddhist traditions, but in a manner that is secularized and devoid of any religious or even spiritual terminology or context. Clinical psychology and psychiatry have even developed a number of therapeutic applications based on Mindfulness for people experiencing a variety of psychological conditions like, for example, depression, stress and drug addiction.

This widespread popularization of meditative techniques has freed meditation from much of its traditional and cultural baggage and therefore made it much more accessible to the secular, rational, modern mindset of Western culture, which is all very good news in terms of broad cultural development. As a result of this popularization more and more people are practicing many different forms of meditation and are meditating for many different reasons. Probably the most common reason these days is the desire to experience a deeper degree of peace, relaxation and relief from the fast-paced stress of modern life. This is very understandable and Mindfulness meditation can indeed deliver those benefits along with many others that positively impact our physical and psychological health.

While many people practice some kind of meditation technique to experience some degree of peace, relaxation or relief from stress in the midst of the conventional pattern of the first Great Search that I have already described, it is only when we have begun to traverse the Crossroads of positive disillusionment, and are receptive to the pure longing of the Fire of the Heart, that meditation can be truly approached as a Direct Door to Awakening.

When we choose to open our hearts and minds to the Infinite and dare to consider the fundamental questions of existence – Who are we? Why are we here? What is our Source and what is our relationship to it? – we begin to Awaken from the very convincing dream of separate selfhood that is embedded in our unconscious identification with an individual body-mind. Our first initiation into Awakening may be an undeniable Glimpse, like being in a darkened room and opening a door very slightly that reveals a penetrating crack of Light. Or it may happen in a more dramatic way, when the door suddenly swings wide open and our entire "room" is suddenly ablaze with luminosity. The inrush of Light may even be so overwhelming that the walls of our "room" fall out, the doors and windows disappear and there is no separateness or difference or sense of limitation whatsoever. But regardless of whether it is a quietly penetrating Glimpse of liberating insight, or a full-blown Revelation of Awakened Consciousness, usually, suddenly or gradually, the door closes again. However, if we have reached that point in our evolutionary development in which we are traversing the Crossroads of positive disillusionment, we will never be able to completely forget that Light and what it revealed – the unalloyed Happiness, Freedom, Peace and Fullness of our True Nature.

If the longing for Liberation, for the Fire of the Heart, is truly burning bright, and an unequivocal initiation into Awakening has occurred, then our motive shifts from pursuing a goal of temporarily feeling better to becoming much more interested in freeing ourselves from the conditioned activity of the ego "I" that is the source of *all* of our unnecessary stress, existential tension and conflicted experience of separation and limitation. Rather than seeking to temporarily smother the discontent of the suffering ego "I", and pacify our mind through some fleeting "high" or "peak" experience, we are now ready and willing to give ourselves to the necessary *discipline and practice* that will enable us to deepen and embody that Awakening Consciousness that is calling us forward.

Then we are ripe and ready to engage with what I will simply call the practice of True Meditation. When I refer to True Meditation as a practice I don't mean the repetitive doing of something until one becomes good at it or perfects it, as the word "practice" usually implies, and nor do I mean the application of a particular technique. As you will see True Meditation can be engaged in formal periods of sitting practice, but it is not necessarily limited to any particular period of formal meditation "practice time". What my instructions will be pointing toward is a potential discovery of our True Nature *here and now* that can organically permeate our essential disposition in relationship to all of life.

Therefore True Meditation is not an *incremental* means to *become* Free, Happy and Peaceful step by step sometime in the future, it is a potentially *radical* means to Awaken to our *already* Free, Happy and Peaceful True Nature *right now*. Thus in the context of this understanding, I like to describe True Meditation as the Practice of Awakening.

# Chapter 10

# Preparation for Meditation

Before entering into the practice of meditation and indeed any spiritual practice, it is important to be prepared in the right manner. If you are a beginner to meditation practice what follows is essential reading, but if you are already engaged in a regular meditation practice then most, or perhaps all, of what I cover in this chapter may already be familiar to you. However, I still recommend reading it as you may also find some pointers that will help to keep you on track.

## How to Sit

In meditation one ideally wants to be able to let go of bodily tensions and relax completely, so a stable sitting posture is essential. You want to sit in a posture that will enable you to sit comfortably without moving for twenty minutes minimum and up to an hour for a longer session of meditation. There are three basic postures you can choose from to meditate. Sitting on the floor cross-legged on a cushion, kneeling on a cushion or a small bench (often called Zen or Japanese style) or sitting on a chair. For all these postures the most important thing is to make sure that you can sit comfortably with your back straight and your head upright.

To sit crosslegged on the floor with a straight back, you will need to sit with your knees lower than your hips. If you are flexible enough you can meditate in a half lotus pose with the legs crossed and one foot resting, sole upwards, on the opposite thigh. In all postures, sitting on the floor, kneeling or sitting on a chair, the hands should be folded on the lap, or resting on the knees, with palms upward or downward. It may also be helpful to have the thumb and index finger of each hand touching lightly. In this way the circuit of energy in the body remains closed and balanced.

If you sit in a chair make sure that it is firm and not too soft. Make sure to sit straight; you can cross the legs at the ankles if you want but not at the knees. Do not lean into the back of the chair for support, but sit erect so that the body supports itself.

Generally try to sit on a cushion made of natural fibers or a wooden bench placed on a blanket, rug, or mat, also made of natural fibers. Such materials naturally conduct the flow of energy between the body and the earth, while synthetic materials may cut off or obstruct this flow.

Most people are drawn to meditate with eyes closed, but you can experiment with meditating with eyes open as the Zen Buddhists do. If you meditate with eyes open simply look forward and slightly downward with an open relaxed gaze. Decide before a session of meditation if you will meditate with eyes closed or eyes open and do not switch back and forth during the session. If you choose to meditate with eyes open it is important that you do not allow yourself to get distracted or fascinated by whatever is appearing in your visual field.

## When to Practice

Avoid sitting in meditation immediately after eating, otherwise you are likely to experience sleepiness and dullness. Wait until the digestive processes have settled and the circulation of the life force has returned to the whole body after its temporary concentration on digestion. It is best to practice meditation at times when you are refreshed and relaxed and free from outer obligations. If possible practice meditation at the same time each day. Early morning before you get involved with your daily activities is best, but in the early evening after work and before dinner may also be an optimal time. When you have a day free from obligations take the opportunity to meditate more frequently and perhaps also occasionally spend an entire day in silence in between meditation sessions.

For a formal committed practice I recommend that you meditate once or twice a day in a quiet place where you can relax and be free from distraction. If you can meditate in the same place everyday, and if you have a space that you can devote only to meditation practice, then this is ideal. Keep the space clean and perhaps grace it with flowers and incense. If you feel moved to create some kind of shrine you could include a Buddha statue or images of any other Spiritual Masters that you are inspired by, or if you prefer to have none of this and gravitate toward a clean, uncluttered space that is also fine. You should simply go with your own intuitive resonance in this matter.

What is of paramount importance is that you are sincere in your longing to Awaken and that you make your meditation practice a priority in your life and practice with consistency. Sitting for twenty minutes each day is far more effective than meditating for an hour once or twice a week.

## Dealing with Resistance

In the beginning you are likely to experience resistance to establishing a committed practice. You will be tempted to not do it when you do not feel like it, and you will probably find yourself making excuses for not keeping your commitment. Then you will try to fit the practice in around other activities in your daily life and meditation will gradually drop down the list of priorities. This is why your longing for liberation, the Fire of the Heart, is the most important ingredient on your journey, for only then will you have the clarity of intention necessary to prevail against the obstacles and temptations that your ego "I" will throw up in an effort to sabotage your commitment to the Awakening Process.

Once you are sitting in meditation the most obvious way that resistance will arise is through wanting to move, whether due to some physical pain or discomfort or simply because you are not accustomed to sitting still. When you make a commitment to be still for a period of time, to access the dimension of yourself that never moves, then the part of you that is never still will become agitated. The ego "I" is not interested in, and is often threatened by, stillness or inactivity. In the modern West, and increasingly all over the world, we are culturally conditioned and wired for speed, stimulation and agitation. So before you identify with the temptation to move during meditation ask yourself: Am I agitated? Am I afraid? Am I contracted in my body? If the answer is yes then take this opportunity to see the resistance to stillness that is arising in you. Breathe and release it, observe it, see and feel through it, bear the discomfort and then decide if you really need to move or not. Meditation is an opportunity to clearly see the movement of the ego "I" for what it is. If you want to liberate yourself then you must observe what is at the root of the impulse to move and then make the effort to not move. If you can do this you may find that the pain in your body, or the anxiety and the tension that was so present just seconds ago, has fallen away. And even if those unpleasant sensations do not fall away it may not matter, because you will be immersed in the deep stillness that is the essential "you" that is only accessible when "you" are not attached to or fascinated by the fear, anxiety and the agitation of the conditioned mind.

If you have the opportunity to meditate in a group, which I highly recommend, be aware of what happens to others when you move or to you when others move. Notice that when you move usually someone else also moves. Notice when someone else moves that the pull in you to move gets stronger. See how one person moving in meditation can affect the stillness of the group as a whole. You must decide if you really need to move. If you do decide to move then move as consciously and as quietly as possible. Take the time to contemplate this between your meditations so you will be ready if and when resistance to stillness arises in your next meditation.

Another form of resistance that commonly manifests once you have sat down to meditate is dullness and sleepiness. If you are very physically tired then it is best not to meditate. One of the reasons why meditating on rising first thing in the morning is preferable is because you are fresh from a night's sleep, and you have not yet gotten involved with the tasks and demands of your day. But even if you are not physically tired you may find that when you sit down to meditate you are overcome by drowsiness and find yourself repeatedly nodding off. This is when you can know that you are encountering resistance. The drowsiness and dullness that you may be experiencing have nothing to do with actually needing more sleep. It is simply the momentum of your ego "I" that does not want to become more conscious, that does not want to Awaken.

The only way to deal with this form of resistance is to make consistent effort to pay attention regardless of the sleepiness. If you are still struggling even when making effort to pay attention, then I suggest that you meditate with open eyes. If sleepiness is a strong tendency in you it may take a period of consistent determined practice of making the effort to stay awake to make a breakthrough. But if you persist you will eventually break the momentum of that deeply conditioned pull toward dullness and drowsiness, and then you will find that you can stay alert and awake more effortlessly.

# Chapter 11

# The Breath of Life

ONCE you are sitting comfortably in one of the three postures I have suggested the first thing to do is to make sure that you are breathing freely without any obstruction. That means breathing all the way in and down, so that your abdomen expands slightly as you breathe. It is helpful to take a few deep breaths at the beginning of a meditation session to establish this rhythm, but you do not have to continue to take deep breaths after that, you only need to make sure that your breathing is complete and free from tension.

Many of us do not breathe fully and freely. We tend to breathe very shallowly, only breathing into the lungs and chest area. As a result we are hardly ever deeply at ease, even when we are inactive. So make sure your abdomen expands slightly as you breath in. Once you give a little attention to this rhythm of breathing it will soon become effortless, for this is how the body naturally wants to breathe.

In the physics of the different dimensions of our being, ether or energy is the subtlest of the gross elements, which also include, solid, liquid, fiery and gaseous substances. Ether is the all-pervading element of the physical universe, analogous to space itself. The etheric dimension pervades and surrounds the universe and all bodies. It is the field of energy, magnetism and space in which the grosser elements function. Thus it serves as a conduit for the forces of universal light and energy to animate the physical body. Our etheric or energy body correlates to the dimension of vitality and life force, and is a subtle medium between the conscious mind and the physical body that primarily functions through the nervous system.

We tend to assume that the principal source of energy for the physical body is food, but it is the agency of breathed vitality that enables us to assimilate and convert food. The breath cycle is the interface between consciousness and energy, the vehicle by which the etheric substance of universal life force is communicated to and distributed throughout the body. So when we breathe we are in actuality feeding directly on universal life energy.

*****

Begin with what I call the "I AM Breath". As you inhale simply say inwardly "I" and as you exhale say "AM". You can do this for as long as you feel drawn to do it, and then simply let it go and be with the sensation and flow of the breath.

As you breathe allow yourself to yield in open delight to your embodiment and the flow of life force that is generated through the sensation of the inhalation and exhalation. Observe what happens at the end of an exhalation. Be aware of the still point as the exhalation ends and before the inhalation begins. Where does it go? What does it disappear into? Then shift your attention to the beginning of the inhalation and be aware of its source. Where does the breath come from? What causes it to come into being? What initiates it? Of course there will not be a mental answer to these questions, but simply asking them will facilitate a deeper intimacy and sense of merging with the breath.

Through simply being attentive, receptive, and curious as you observe the body breathing, any tension that you are carrying will gradually unwind into deep relaxation. As you merge your awareness more and more deeply with the flow of the breath, you will become tacitly aware that "you" are not breathing; rather you are being breathed. Breathing is always with you; it is the pulsation of Life itself animating your physical form.

Open to the presence and energy of this Life force. Allow gratitude for the miracle of the Breath of Life that animates your embodiment to radiate throughout your entire being. With every breath you take you are surrendering to that Power, Process or Being that truly "lives" you and everything that exists.

Of course your mind may not easily cooperate with the simplicity and focus of this meditation, but that does not matter at all. Every time that you get distracted by thinking about the past or future, about this or that, simply and gently bring your attention back to observing and following the sensation and movement of the body breathing as I have described.

Be patient and the mind will calm down. There is a connection between the breath and the mind. Thought and respiration are different aspects of the same "life-current" upon which both depend. Through this meditation on the breath the mind is detached from other activities and engaged in watching the breath. As your breathing slows down and becomes smooth and regular, your mind also will become calm and one pointed.

If you are feeling particularly agitated and easily distracted I suggest that you focus on a particular aspect of the breathing, like the rise and fall of your belly, or the sensation of the air going in and out through the nostrils. If you tend to be a characteristically "airy" and ungrounded person, then I suggest focusing on the belly. If you tend to be a characteristically "solid" or "earthy" person, then I suggest focusing on the flow of the breath as it enters and exits the nostrils. But regardless of whether you focus your attention on one point or on the entire flow of the respiratory process, the most important thing is that you have infinite patience and simply keep bringing your attention back to the breath. If you continually get distracted simply let go of any expectations, frustrations or struggle that may arise and be here and now with the sensation and movement of the body breathing to the best of your ability. Continue to bring yourself back to the breath, that is all you need to do.

If you practice in this way with sincerity and consistency the tensions and constrictions in your psychophysical being will gradually uncoil into deeper levels of relaxation and, at the same time, you will develop a calm centeredness and concentration in which you are simultaneously very alert and awake. You will start to feel fundamentally grounded and content to sit still and simply *be*.

By "grounded and content" I do not mean that your mind is always quiet or that you are only experiencing pleasant feelings. I simply mean that you are at ease with being still and attentive to the breath, and that you are not experiencing strong resistance, regardless of what is arising. Even if you are experiencing some form of resistance to being still and attentive to the breath you are not making the experience of resistance into a problem. You are simply content and at ease.

*****

This form of meditation is often called "Mindfulness of Breathing" in Buddhist and Mindfulness circles, but I prefer to call it the "Breath of Life". The word "mindfulness", because of its association with "mind", tends to lack the quality of deep feeling and surrender. In my opinion a better translation would be "feeling awareness" or "feeling attention". Including this aspect of feeling is important, because if meditation is going to be a vehicle for authentic Awakening it is essential that we bring the component of devotion and love to it.

I was once asked by a participant attending one of my meditation retreats about the difference between meditation and prayer. I surprised myself by saying that ultimately they are the same thing. The reason I surprised myself is that, like most of us growing up with a Christian background, I had always associated prayer with "petitionary" prayer, a dualistic "dialogue" between one's inner "I" and the perceived sense of an external God. But the reason I said that they are the same is because when one drops the dualistic form of petitionary prayer and offers the totality of one's being as a prayer to the "Living" God – God as an ever-present Great Mystery – then this gesture of devotional sacrifice of the inward "I" ultimately brings one into heartfelt meditation. So allow your meditation to become a prayer. Then you do not simply observe the breath "at a distance", but you also *feel* your oneness with the breath and the flowing radiance of the life current throughout your whole body and beyond.

Meditation on the Breath of Life is the most simple and direct form of meditation on an object. There are many other forms of meditation on an object, including the use of various mantras or visualizations or meditative techniques that involve the manipulation of attention and energy, but this is the most simple and accessible form. The bare simplicity of the breath is less esoteric than other possible objects of meditation, and so one cannot practice a more down-to-earth and grounding form of meditation on an object. This utterly simple meditative approach is always available. You do not have to be initiated into any kind of complex esoteric practice to meditate on the Breath of Life, and spiritual aspirants throughout the centuries have practiced it. Indeed, it is the form of meditation on an object that was taught by Gautama Buddha himself 2500 (more or less) years ago.

*****

You can think of the Breath of Life as creating an anchor not only for meditation practice, but also for your entire functional being. Practicing the Breath of Life will bring the conditions of mind, emotion and body into fundamental alignment and balance. This is something that I suggest that you do artfully at any time randomly throughout your day, especially when you are feeling under stress. You don't have to be sitting down in meditation to do this. You can simply bring your attention to breathing fully and completely. Diet, exercise and other disciplines also contribute to healthy balanced functioning, but full and unobstructed breathing is more essential to our fundamental well being than most of us realize. The quality of our breathing has a significant impact on the cycles of stress and reactive emotions. If you become aware of breathing as a constant full process of energy and feeling, then you will discover that disciplining of your emotional and physical life will become more and more effortless. And if you are experiencing challenging and agitated emotions like anger or fear, if you simply take a full belly breath you will be amazed at how quickly those emotions dissipate and fall away.

Once you are able to meditate on the Breath of Life with ease for sessions of forty-five minutes to an hour, and you feel consistently content in the way I have described above, then you are ready to take the next step, which is meditation *without an object*. However, even if you are ready to move on I recommend that you always begin your meditation session with this practice of the Breath of Life for at least the first few minutes to establish yourself in equanimity and the free flow of life energy. Then, as you relinquish your one pointed focus on the Breath of Life, you remain in the inner posture of surrender to the Mystery that lies behind Life and from which Life springs, which is Consciousness Itself.

# Chapter 12

# Letting Everything Be As It Is

Once you feel established in a fundamental sense of ease and contentment through practicing the Breath of Life, I encourage you to gently let go of focusing on your object – the movement and sensation of the breath in this case – and allow your awareness to open and expand into meditation without an object. To do this you simply let go of focusing on anything at all, which means we relinquish the *act of giving attention to anything in particular.*

The act of attention is the motivating principle of mind. What you pay attention to becomes who you are and defines your experience. Without paying attention to something you cannot know it. While our five senses provide us with information about the world, we can only know that information by attending to it. If we do not pay attention to the information provided we can fail to see something that happens right in front of our eyes or to hear the conversation of two people sitting next to us.

If you have practiced any self-observation at all you have probably noticed that you tend to experience and enact what you give your attention to. If you focus on perceived injustice you feel resentful and angry, if you focus on sexual fantasies you become sexually aroused, if you focus on your worries about the future you become afraid, if you focus on loss you become sorrowful and so forth. So if we want to go beyond that mundane self-contracted activity of the ego "I", we have to become responsible for the act of attention itself, otherwise we will remain bound and distracted by the conditioned force of egoic habits. Because Consciousness is not an object what we need to do to obtain clear knowledge is withdraw our attention from all the objects known by our attention.

True Meditation is the practice of relinquishing fixation on any phenomenal experience. The way that this is approached is by simply letting everything that arises – every sensation, feeling, thought and perception – be exactly *as it is*, free from desire, fear, judgement and manipulation of any kind whatsoever.

Meditation without an object is a greater challenge than meditation on an object, because if we have an object to focus on then at least we have something to do! We have a method or technique to practice and so we have something to direct our attention towards. Meditation on the Breath of Life can help to ground us in the present moment and free our awareness from aimless distraction. By focusing our attention one pointedly on the movement and sensation of the breathing, to the exclusion of all other objects, we can develop a state of meditative concentration that can lead us into a peaceful "deeper" state of consciousness. Yet as peaceful and profound as such states may be, if we want to discover who we really are *prior to and beyond all states*, beyond all the permutations of experience high and low, then we need to let go of our attachment to any particular state, and our dependence on any particular technique.

*****

While reflecting one day on all that I had learned in almost thirty years of consistent meditation practice, and in a few years of teaching meditation, I wrote down a set of instructions for the participants of my retreats:

*Sitting still, relaxing deeply, alert and awake*
*I let everything be exactly as it is.*
*With no problem, no expectation and no struggle*
*I meditate with infinite patience.*
*With nothing to do, nothing to change, nothing to achieve,*
*Free from identification with the arising of thought,*
*I simply rest as Consciousness itself.*

These instructions are my own articulation of the most essential and direct form of meditation, which can be found in some form at the mystical heart of most spiritual traditions – meditation on Consciousness Itself. It is this absolutely simple yet profound practice of objectless meditation that is a direct doorway to Awakening.

As I made clear earlier, because it does not involve any technique, this meditation is not a practice in the sense of the repetitive doing of something until one becomes good at it or perfects it. What these instructions are pointing to is the potential discovery of our Being-Consciousness that is *always already* the case.

The first line of instruction is a simple description of the inner posture of True Meditation practice and the spiritually Awakened Condition:

*Sitting still, relaxing deeply, alert and awake*

If you are resting in the basic equanimity of meditation then the poles of passivity (relaxation) and activity (alertness) merge and become one and the same. If you are feeling dull or sleepy or aimlessly distracted, then you are veering too far toward the passive pole and you need to engage in a degree of "noble effort", as Gautama Buddha called it, to be more alert and present. On the other hand, if you are too tense and effortful in your approach, you need to relax into a more receptive mode. Once you find that middle place beyond this pair of opposites you will know it, because it is your inherently Natural State. It is like trying to direct a thread through the eye of a needle. It might take some adjustment, but once the thread is through, there is an inward sense of "Ah that's it" and then you just know it, and you can let go and allow yourself to come to rest.

It can be helpful to envision what I am describing as "coming to rest" as resting in and as the "Heart" I was describing earlier, which is not the physical heart, but the spiritual Heart that is your deepest intuited True Nature. The Heart of the title of this book represents the Infinite and Radiant Consciousness that is the very Nature and

Condition of all beings and things. Although it may be intuited at the physical heart, the spiritual Heart is not located inside the body and mind, nor is it located in any place in relation to the body and mind. As we will discover the body and mind arise within that all-pervading Consciousness, or Heart.

*****

Once you are resting in a disposition of relaxed, open alertness, then engage the next line of the instructions:

*I let everything be exactly as it is*

This simple phrase epitomizes the essence of True Meditation and all of the instructions I am sharing could be distilled down to this simple single sentence. The practice of *letting everything be as it is* simply means that we detach from the habitual wandering attention of the ego "I" and rest in the position of what is often called "the Witness".

The Witness refers to our fundamental experience of being conscious before we identify with anything. It is that Being-Consciousness, that I AM Presence, that we *always already* ARE, that is the essential fact and knowing of our existence. Resting as the Witness we *already* see, feel and know, without any reflection, motive or effort of any kind whatsoever. As the Witness we perceive everything, and yet we are untouched by anything; this is why it is often described as the "mirror mind" in Buddhist literature. We simply see without interpretation. We simply know without knowing. We are simply conscious without being self-conscious. Your essential experience of being conscious right now *is* IT. Before you take any point of view, and have any particular relationship to your experience, you are simply aware of everything *as it is*. That is the Witness or Witnessing Consciousness, or the I AM Presence, which we began exploring earlier in the chapter *I AM*.

The key distinction to understand here is that attention is motivated and witnessing is motiveless. You, as the Witness, do not do anything. You do not direct attention toward anything in particular, you simply ARE. You do not have to "try" to be the Witness, because you already *are* the Witness. So watch out for any subtle sense of "trying" to be the Witness that may creep in. We are all addicted to doing, doing, doing by tendency, so even if we are sitting still outwardly, inwardly we can still be busy "watching, watching, watching", being the one who is diligently meditating. The challenge of True Meditation is to let go of all self-conscious control, which means to relinquish all strategic approaches through techniques and methodologies.

*****

No matter what arises, whether pleasant or unpleasant, you resolve to simply let everything be *as it is*. However, when you attempt to let everything be as it is, you will almost definitely discover that you don't want to do it. An enormous momentum has been generated by the constant repetition of your past habits of attention – your fascinations, your likes and dislikes, and all your worries and problems – and this momentum makes it appear as if your mind and emotions are tormenting you. But if you truly aspire to Awaken to a deeper dimension of Being you will resolve to rest in and as the Witness no matter how many times you appear to get lost.

If you simply and gently persist in letting everything be as it is, and letting everything be as it is, and letting everything be as it is, and every time that you notice that you have become identified with a train of thought, then you simply let *that* be as it is and step off the thought train, you will eventually discover space. You will recognize over and over and over again that the mechanism of self-identification with your psychological experience is, and always has been, your *own activity*. This consistent recognition and relinquishment of every movement of identification with any object that arises progressively enables you to let every thought, and every emotion, and every sensation, be *as it is* no matter what.

*****

True Happiness, Peace, Freedom and Fulfillment can only be discovered through surrender, only through letting go absolutely, not through "doing" anything. This is why True Meditation cannot be reduced to a technique. You, the meditator, cannot do it. Rather you, the meditator, must be *undone*. This is a maddening double bind for the ego "I" that always wants to be the "doer", and you will no doubt keep getting caught up in that double bind of trying to be the one who is doing the meditation. But even if that double bind is arising you can let *that* be as it is also! Then the double bind will dissolve and cease to be an impediment to letting everything be as it is. The good news here is that no matter how lost you *appear* to get in the convoluted ups and downs of your mental and emotional experience, it is never too late to let everything be exactly as it is.

While True Meditation may not be easy to practice initially, if your longing for Liberation is profound, and your commitment to practice is consistent, you will progressively become more and more capable of this surrender. If your approach to meditation practice is sincere you will not be meditating in order to get something out of your experience, or to exploit your experience in some way. Rather you will be more interested in discovering the potential for radical liberation *from* all experience. Therefore, you will not be attracted to dwelling on the past, internally dramatizing personal problems, or indulging in future fantasies. Such things may arise, but you will not be compelled to give them your energy and attention. You will be less interested in the self-defeating process of *trying* to observe and control everything, and you will be more attracted toward surrender, toward release, toward the directly intuited Mystery of Consciousness Itself.

If there is sincere aspiration, then the inner attitude or posture of True Meditation is one of profound self-forgetting, surrender, and sacrifice of our habitual narcissistic focus on the highs and lows of our psychological experience. We yield the totality of ourselves to that unseen Mystery or Presence that is our deepest intuited nature. In so doing we free our attention and energy from the self-contraction that is defined by moment-to-moment identification with the body-mind. This posture of self-surrender must be as constant as possible throughout our meditation, and indeed throughout our entire life, so that we are continuously able to rediscover the ever-present ground of Spiritual Freedom here and now.

# Chapter 13

# No Problem

*With no problem, no expectation and no struggle*

*I meditate with infinite patience.*

*With nothing to do, nothing to change, nothing to achieve*

Another way to language the instruction "let everything be as it is" is to say "simply practice having no problem in relationship to anything that arises". This description challenges us to let go of our insistence on any problem, dilemma, block or obstacle of any kind...*from the very beginning!* So as you sit quietly, deeply relaxed, alert and awake, simply resolve to not make a problem out of anything that arises, no matter how disturbing or unpleasant it may be.

By assuming the posture of "no problem" you will simultaneously be letting go of any expectations about what should or should not happen in your meditation. If there is no problem and you have no expectations, then it follows that you will not be struggling with your psychological experience. Your mind may be very agitated, there may be doubting thoughts, crazy thoughts or mundane thoughts arising, you may be experiencing difficult emotions and memories, but still you do not struggle with or against any of them, because you have resolved to remain relaxed and alert in your posture of "no problem" and "no expectation" and letting everything be.

As you let everything be as it is in this way, you will feel the existential tension that you habitually carry in your psychophysical system beginning to uncoil, as you did when you were practicing the Breath of Life. But now an even greater depth of ease and relaxation can be experienced because you are relinquishing *all* doing. You will discover an expansive pool of infinite space in relationship to the shifting flux of your psychological experience, no matter how challenging it may appear to be at times. When you genuinely let go of trying to do anything with your experience, of trying to manipulate or change your experience in any way, then you will simultaneously find that you have let go of any desire to achieve anything at all. You have let go of any time-bound relationship to meditation, any idea that meditation is about moving from whatever state you might be experiencing now, to a "higher" or more "spiritual" state somewhere in the future. You realize that there is only one moment and that moment is now. *This is It!*

*****

Deeply discovering the truth of no problem has radical implications not only for our meditation practice, but also for our entire life. Ask yourself: Is there ever *really* a problem? If you let everything be as it is in this or any moment the whole notion of a "problem" has no meaning. As soon as you look for the problem or block, you will realize that it has no substance. But this fact is obscured by our more or less continuous *presumption* of a problem, of something *already* being wrong or missing from this moment.

If we let everything be as it is, we will see that that presumption is our *own activity*. The so-called problem never actually arises, and it becomes clear that we create it. It is the attachment of the ego "I" to its felt sense of lack, to its desires and fears, and its conceptions of "right" and "wrong", and "good" and "bad", and "should" and "should not", that creates the notion of a problem.

In Reality – by which I mean what IS when we take the projections of the ego "I" out of the picture – there is only the arising of phenomena. Some of those conditions may be painful in various ways, and we may feel compelled to change them, but if we are established in the posture of no problem then our action will spring from allowing everything to be as it is *first*. Then we are not in a disposition of problematic avoidance, reaction or struggle with what is. On the contrary we are in direct relationship with what is, and discover that we are able to respond creatively to life's challenges, rather than reacting mechanically to them.

The moment of letting go is immediate release from the bondage of any problem or dilemma. We are not liberated because "we" solved something. Rather Liberation is simply spontaneous non-verbal understanding of *what is*, which is identical to Reality or Consciousness Itself. We "stand under", or submit to, the truth of what is, *as it is*, here and now. And in that radical understanding or surrender, there is the simultaneous dissolution of the whirlpool of the ego "I". But if we do not under-stand, if we resist what is, if we continue to assert our sense of independent self-existence in reaction to what is, our projection of what "I" want, or what "I" think should or should not be happening, then our problem, our suffering appears to exist and persist.

*****

See that your habitual suffering is only something that you presume, but that you cannot actually find. To let this in very deeply is to discover that all of the habitual strategies that you have developed in your pursuit of Happiness and Fulfillment are *completely unnecessary*. When there is not the slightest impulse to believe in the binding force of any experience, high or low, then the ego "I" is undone, is dissolved, and is seen through. Then we see with new eyes – and a new "I" – that is washed clean in the baptism of Truth.

In that ever-new baptism of Truth we see both the utter absurdity of the human condition, and the utter seriousness of it. Absurd, because we realize that we were *never* truly stuck, bound or separate in the first place, and that indeed everybody is *already* Free at Heart, if only they could simply *be* and *see*. And serious, because we perceive like never before, the immense veiling power and momentum of human ignorance that is the root cause of so much unbearable, and completely unnecessary suffering.

The Great Search, whether in the form of seeking in the realms of the body, mind and world, or in the form of seeking psychic, subtle and transcendental relief, is what we do when we have *already presumed* that we are a "problem" – a suffering separate knot of self – that needs to be "solved" or "healed". When that presumption dissolves, then prior Freedom and Happiness is revealed to be who we essentially *already* ARE. And if we are ready and willing to let this discovery infuse and permeate all dimensions of our Being very deeply we may smile, laugh, gasp in astonishment, or shed tears of unreasonable, ecstatic joy. Why? Because we unequivocally see that by habit we have been committed to the destiny of separation, suffering and delusion, and yet by Nature we are *already, and always have been, Unified, Happy and Free.*

Let me say that again: by habit we have been committed to the destiny of separation, suffering and delusion, and yet by Nature we are *already, and always have been, Unified, Happy and Free.*

One more time: by habit we have been committed to the destiny of separation, suffering and delusion, and yet by Nature we are *already, and always have been, UNIFIED, HAPPY and FREE!*

# Chapter 14

# Recognition Is Letting Go

THE VERB "to recognize" means to "know again". In relationship to letting everything be as it is that means that in the instant that you "re-cognize" that you are actively and exclusively giving your attention to a particular thought, emotion or sensation (not letting it be as it is) then you simultaneously relinquish that conditioned activity of identification. This act of re-cognition *is* letting go of the self-contraction of the ego "I" moment by moment. It is an instantaneous and nonverbal process of Liberation that, if practiced consistently, potentially becomes an ongoing disposition both in and outside periods of formal meditation.

The specific value of the formal practice period of meditation is that it provides us with an undistracted opportunity to intensify this re-cognition of our own binding activity of self-identification. It is not complex; on the contrary it is radically simple. We re-cognize that our wanting, our resistance, our suffering is always our own event. It is always the theatre of our own action. We understand that we no longer need to go through any sort of complicated affair to be released from our unhappiness. We do not have to go through any kind of therapy, special diet, do some kind of esoteric yoga, concentrate on our third eye, or hum a mantra in order to be Free. All we have to do is let go. Completely. This is the nature of re-cognition. This is what it means to let everything be as it is.

*****

It may be helpful in the earlier stages of practice, or at those times when your mind and emotions are very turbulent, to use an internal verbalization of a phrase from the instructions to facilitate this process. For example, you might simply say to yourself as you are confronting your busy mind, "I let everything be as it is", or when you are experiencing resistance you might bring to mind the phrase, "infinite patience" or "nothing to do". But only do this artfully and at random when it arises spontaneously. Do not make a technique out of it. Then, as you progress, you will find that the process of recognition, of letting everything be, happens more and more spontaneously without any interior verbalization.

*****

The Awakening Process is a journey from complexity to simplicity. By meditating on an object like the utter simplicity of the Breath of Life, we consciously focus our attention on one thing to the exclusion of all other things. Then, through meditation without an object we let go of *all* doing, all activity of motivated attention. We hold onto *nothing*. We allow ourselves to simply BE.

Letting everything BE is absolute simplicity itself, yet because we tend to be complex creatures that are addicted to stimulation, distraction and activity, we resist this radical simplicity. But if we simply allow the resistance that we experience to also be *as it is*, in whatever form it is arising, then we will progressively undermine and displace the controlling activity of the ego "I" from the center of our awareness.

Remember that the ego "I" is the locus of self-contraction that creates the very convincing illusion of independent self-existence. It is the presumed "controller" of experience that sits in the driver's seat of the body-mind entity that we presume ourselves to be. Letting everything be as it is loosens the grip of the ego "I" on the steering wheel, and undermines our need to be in control. And it is this letting go of control that consistently erodes and dissolves the conditioned activity of the ego "I". So if you experience this practice as challenging and difficult, as everyone does at times, and especially in the early and intermediate stages of the Awakening Process, simply understand that it is because of your resistance to letting go of control. And, most importantly, the fact that it is difficult does not mean that you are not doing the practice. It may appear that you are getting "lost" over and over again, but as long as you let everything be as it is, to the best of your ability, as long as you are steadfastly bringing yourself back to the Witness, to the source of your Being, then you are sincerely engaging with the Practice of Awakening.

# Chapter 15

# Consciousness Itself

*Free from identification with the arising of thought,*
*I simply rest as Consciousness itself.*

This instruction does not say, "Free from the arising of thought", it says, "Free from *identification* with the arising of thought". And where it says "thought" you could also include emotion, imagery, or psychophysical phenomena of any kind.

As I hope is clear to you by now, our innate Happiness and Freedom are not found by attempting to eradicate or manipulate our mind, or through denying, resisting or avoiding any aspect of our experience. The Liberation that we seek is paradoxically found by letting go of all preference in relationship to the entire spectrum of our psychophysical experience.

The most common myth about meditation is that it involves the "stopping" of the mind. However, the effort to avoid or escape conceptual thinking is a futile strategy because the effort to stop conceptual thinking only intensifies the self-contraction, which *is* conceptual thinking. Simply close your eyes right now and try to stop your mind and you will see what I mean! Therefore this dilemma is only truly transcended through the constant observation, understanding, and relinquishment of the act of contracted attention itself. In other words, through letting go of all seeking and by letting everything be as it is.

To the degree that we let go of our compulsive attachment to any preference whatsoever, the whirlpool of the ego "I" eventually begins to break up and to slow down. The activity of mind falls away from the foreground of our experience and, regardless of what the mind appears to be doing, we abide as the open space of the Witness. When we completely and resolutely let go of identification and fascination with *all* psychological phenomena we will discover that there is no solid sense of "self" at all, there is only the arising and passing away of experience.

What we habitually experience as a continuous sense of self is the "I" of our self-reference. It is the inner separate "I" that we presume to be the thinker of our thoughts, the feeler of our feelings and the doer of our actions. When the mind is not occupied with creative or practical thoughts, then it comes to rest upon this sense of an inner separate "I" that becomes a kind of default position that is the unquestioned background of our experience. However, as our meditation and exploration into the nature of experience deepens, it becomes more and more obvious that this presumed experiencing entity called "I" is *not* the permanent background of all experience. "My" body, "my" mind, "my" history, "my" qualities, "my" faults are all experiences that arise and fall away. Indeed, any sense of a separate "I" completely shape shifts in dream, and disappears completely when we go into deep sleep every night. And then we quickly reassemble the sense of a separate entity called "I" when we wake up in the morning. Thus we can say that the unexamined sense that all of the passing phenomena of experience point toward a continuous personal "I", that exists independent of them is itself a transient experience that arises and falls away.

The great 20<sup>th</sup> century Indian sage Ramana Maharshi called this presumed separate identity of our habitual self-reference the "I" thought. The "I" thought is the first or primary thought upon which all our other thoughts are strung like beads on the string of a necklace. The primary instruction he gave to cut through the "I" thought, the string of the necklace that glues the illusion of a separate, personal self together, was a method called *atma vichara* in Vedanta. Usually translated as "Self-Inquiry", the *atma vichara* that Ramana recommended was a consistent contemplation on the question, "Who am I?"

All of our life we use the terms "I" and "mine" and "me." We talk about "my" body, "my" mind, "my" family and "my" life. We think we know what the body is, we think we know what a thought is, but do we even know *who* claims to own these things? If this question remains unexamined, we remain trapped in a world of limitation, totally identified with things that have a beginning and an end in time.

Inquiring with the contemplation question, "Who am I?" can be likened to peeling an onion. Every time we ask the question the mind will bring up an answer, for example "I am a man or a woman, I am rich or poor, I am educated or a simple person..." But Ramana encouraged us not to stop with any of these answers, but to keep asking and to keep going deeper. Eventually it becomes clear that all the answers given by the mind to this question are false. We may shift from identifying with the body to identifying with our thoughts, believing that we are the thinking mind, but the mind is also being experienced. We may drop deeper into identification with feelings, but feelings are also being experienced, and they are also passing, coming and going. Finally we come to the fundamental self-concept of "I". So who or what is this "I"? The only answer in the form of a thought that can come is "Me."

If we stay with this "Me", if we try to find it, we may be surprised to discover that it cannot be found. It simply is not there! Yet this moment *is* being experienced, sounds *are* being heard, and form and movement *are* being seen. In the absence of any entity to be found, what remains? Me. This simple practice returns us home to the ungraspable Mystery of who we really are, beyond all definition.

*****

The translation of *atma vichara* as "Self-Inquiry" in English implies a mental process of self-questioning that leads to a recognition of the ungraspable Mystery of the True Self, such as I have just described. However, "atma vichara" can also be translated as "Self-Abidance". So in that sense *atma vichara* is the same as what I am pointing to by using the term "True Meditation". The only difference is that when we sit down to practice True Meditation there is a potentially immediate and direct letting go of all identification with thought, so that we abide in and as Conscious Presence. While in Self-Inquiry the mind is utilized in a contemplative process that ultimately takes one beyond the mind to the recognition of and abidance in that Conscious Presence.

Obviously when we are sitting in meditation we are not doing anything else and so we can potentially let go of all the contents of consciousness. However, we can potentially maintain the flow of meditative awareness throughout all our daily activities by artfully applying *atma vichara* in the form of Self-Inquiry, especially in those moments when we can feel our energy and attention getting attached to objects that cause us to suffer to some degree. Regular periods of formal sitting meditation, combined with this kind of artfully applied contemplation-meditation on the question "Who am I?", always has the power to cut through the whirlpool of the ego "I" and merge us back into abidance as Consciousness Itself.

When we abide more and more consistently in and as Consciousness Itself, then the seemingly personal "I" thought is seen as a derivative of the deeper unchanging impersonal Self that we *really* are. We start to have liberating insight into how the illusion of a separate experiencer that is distinct from the present experience comes from memory, and the rapidity with which our experience of thinking, feeling and sensing changes. We observe how our experience of reality is created from a flow of phenomena in a similar way to how a movie, is created from a rapid succession of snapshots. Our self-identification with this flow of experience creates the illusion of a continuous, personal "I" that is the experiencer of the movie just as the whirling of a burning sparkler on a dark night creates the illusion of a continuous ring of fire.

The more we come to rest in and as the pure I AM Witness that takes no position in relationship to the flow of experience, the more the apparently personal, separate inside "I" is seen and understood to be an *object*, rather than the *subject* of experience. As this understanding deepens through Meditation and Self-Inquiry, the "I" of our habitual self-reference, that we have to use to function in the world (Hello "I" am Peter, how are you?), ceases to be the default position that is always apparently there in between all thoughts and images. The sense of a continuous, separate, personal, inside "I" is seen and understood to simply be another thought or image. Then it becomes more and more natural for us to rest in and as our own Source, which is unknowable as an object, which is boundless and inherently Free. Externally we still inhabit a recognizable physical form and personality that seems more or less consistent from day to day, but inwardly we become much more at ease with not needing to know who we are to fully be who we are. We discover the radically simple yet profound liberation of being nobody.

# Chapter 16

# Radiant Presence

Wᴴᴱɴ we see our habitual sense of a separate, personal, inside "I" as an object rather than the subject, then we let go of the presumption of being the thinker of our thoughts. We realize that, other than when we are consciously engaging with thought for practical or creative reasons, the aimless chatter of thought is not generated by us at all. Thoughts are simply arising, and don't necessarily have anything to do with a presumed thinker. As meditation deepens the mind is experienced like a radio playing, as it meanders disjointedly through the force of its own momentum and occasionally dissolves into nothingness. Whether the radio continues to chatter indefinitely or whether it increasingly disappears, it makes *no difference* to us, for we have chosen not to listen to it and not to feed it with our fascination. Regardless of whether we like the particular song the radio is playing or not, we have *no relationship* with it whatsoever.

As we let everything be as it is, and continue to let everything be as it is, and continue to let everything be as it is, there may be periods in which thought slows down considerably and the gaps between thoughts get bigger. When we become very still we may experience periods of complete emptiness and silence of mind. But we cannot really speak of this as an "experience" because that implies an experiencer. Perhaps it is more accurate to describe it as an "absence". We find that who or whatever we habitually think we are dissolves, as we fall into ever widening depths of timeless, formless, blissful Being. This can be likened to slowly sinking to the bottom of the ocean with the flickering mind-waves above fading further and further from view.

As we gently land on the ocean floor, the subtle awareness of "witnessing" also falls away. When that happens our abidance as the Witness transmutes into a seamless Presence in which the subtle duality of the witness and the witnessed, of subject and object, dissolves. The apparent meditator dissolves completely into meditation. Awash in the boundless Freedom of having nothing, knowing nothing and being nobody, we rest in and as the deeply blissful radiant Presence of Consciousness Itself.

*****

As your immersion in True Meditation matures over time you will more and more consistently rest in and as the I AM Witness, not only when you are sitting on your meditation cushion, but also throughout the changing events and circumstances of your life. And on occasion, you may increasingly experience the sense of witnessing spontaneously dissolving into Non-Dual Presence. Your experience of your individual body-mind then abides more and more in the "not knowing" of Consciousness Itself that is infused with a luminous Radiance.

If you give yourself wholeheartedly to the Fire of the Heart and to

True Meditation, then a moment will come in which you will realize with penetrating clarity that the "I" of your self-reference, the personal "I" that you had always presumed that you were, *never actually existed*.

In that depth you discover a profound Peace, but not merely the peace of a "quiet mind" – although the mind may indeed dissolve into pure absence and silence at times – rather you discover what St. Paul is said to have described as the "Peace that passeth all understanding". That Peace is not just the absence of disturbance, or a "feeling" of calm and contentment. It is a Peace that radically transcends and includes all the phenomena of lived experience.

This Peace is also what the Buddhists mean by the concept of "emptiness", which points to an inconceivable Mystery beyond all concepts, all subject-object distinctions and all pairs of opposites. Usually the concept of emptiness is equated with the idea of "no mind" in the sense of "nothing arising" but its true meaning is much more subtle.

Emptiness means that everything that arises is seen as "empty" of self-nature, and therefore as inherently non-binding. Whether there is the non-arising or arising of phenomena, there is ultimately *no difference*. This understanding results in the Peace that is represented by Gautama Buddha sitting in meditation in perfect equilibrium with a gentle smile on his face. When we let go of the illusion of independent self-existence *completely*, when we want *nothing* and resist *nothing*, this profound Peace miraculously reveals itself like the softly penetrating rays of the dawning sun falling upon our face, and awakening us from our dream of separate selfhood.

That essential Peace, that deep well of Mystery, is the True Being behind the "I" of my, your and everybody's self-reference. It is the "I" that is looking out of the eyes of everyone that you see. It is the One who is always already *being* the "I", not the one who merely refers to him or her self as a separate, distinct, historical "I" called Peter, Mary or John. Then "I" understand that "I" am being lived by that Great One, even though "I" can never know what IT is or what I AM. Thus, when we release our habitual identification with the time-bound, skin-encapsulated, historical, suffering and limited ego "I", we discover ourselves resting in and as that unfathomable Radiance of Mystery.

## *I simply rest as Consciousness Itself*

We dis-cover that essential timeless Being, Peace and Happiness that *is*, and *has always been*, and *eternally will be* our True Self, always and forever shining through the relative appearances and the highs and the lows, of phenomenal experience, now and now and now.

# Part IV

# THE SECRET OF FREEDOM

# Chapter 17

# Always Already Free

Wʜᴇɴ we have no awareness of our True Nature as Consciousness, then the body-mind in which we appear to be encapsulated represents the past moving into the future. Because we are too busy surviving and continuing as the person we presume ourselves to be, we have little real awareness of the present. The momentum of our conditioned patterning is so strong that we tend to miss it, we have no time for it, because we are so occupied with the experiences we are having and all the implications of the arising phenomena of the world. However, if we regularly put into practice the simple instructions I have described then every time that we sit down to meditate, or indeed at any moment when we relinquish our habitual activity of fascination and identification with the whirlpool of the ego "I", we will potentially merge into the ever-new open secret of the Transcendental Reality of Consciousness Itself.

The radical nature of Consciousness Itself *always already* IS regardless of what seems to be arising inwardly or outwardly in the world of phenomenal experience. Before we recognize that deepest truth and ground of who we really are, and whether we recognize it or not, it is *always already* the case. Consciousness, Spirit, God, the Supreme Identity, whatever name we want to give the unnamable wonder of existence, simply *IS*. It is the Great Context in which all contents, including our individuated body-minds and this multitudinous display of manifestation, appear. It is always here and now *as* YOU, waiting to be re-cognized or known again in every moment. That is the miracle and the perennial "good news" of Awakening.

When we discover this miracle, whether it is for the first time or for the umpteenth time, it is always fresh and *ever new*. Again and again we re-cognize, meaning that we know again, this wonder-full secret that is apparently hidden in plain sight. When we are willing to let absolutely everything be as it is, when we are willing to surrender our seeking, our fear and our resistance, then we acknowledge and accept the Presence of Consciousness, of Spirit, of Divine Radiance at this very moment. This acknowledgement is the radical acceptance that everything is as it is *because it is*. There is only one moment and *this is It*. There is no fundamental dilemma, problem or anything missing from the inherent perfection of this moment now.

When we truly let go of wanting our experience to be a particular way, we recognize that absolutely everything that happens is *already* the way it is. So it is not even really a matter of us "accepting" what is, because what is *already* is, whether we like it or not! Even if we are struggling to let everything be, that is the way it is. Even if our mind is telling us that we cannot meditate, that we are doing it wrong, that we are useless, and that we might as well give up all this spiritual awakening business, *that is the way it is*. Even if we are repeatedly getting lost in daydreams and fantasies...*that is the way it is*. When we truly allow ourselves to accept what is, *as it is*, free from any movement of desiring what is *not* here and now, or resisting what *is* here and now, the seed of seeking is dissolved in its Source and the spell of the inward turning suffering whirlpool of the ego "I" is broken.

Letting everything be as it is brings us to the direct recognition of who we always already ARE. Letting go liberates us spontaneously from the illusion of separation and limitation created by our habitual identification with the movements of desire and fear. When we surrender to the Truth that this moment is the *only* moment, then we discover that the Consciousness that we are looking *for* is the One that is *always already looking*.

Practice letting everything be as it is consistently, when you are meditating, when you are walking, when you are sitting on the bus, at any moment through your day, and you will re-cognize over and over again, that it is only your usually unconscious and unexamined identification with your mind and emotions that creates a problem with what is, and that is why you try to solve or manipulate your experience in some way, shape or form. The moment "you" presume that "something is wrong" with "you" or "your" experience, then that imagined entity called "you" creates the whirlpool of the ego "I", turning in upon itself, addicted to its own self-importance and oblivious to the wider ocean of Being.

*****

Because Consciousness is *always already* the case whether you realize it or not, Awakening always comes in the form of an immediate shift in perception. It is not you as an individual that Awakens. The "You" that wakes up from the dream of independent self-existence is not the "you" of your historical story. You do not awaken to something; rather Consciousness Awakens to Itself. It discovers Itself. Awakening Awakens! And when Awakening Awakens it seems so obvious that we wonder how we could ever have missed it.

You will save yourself a lot time and suffering in the Awakening Process if you are willing to acknowledge and accept that the ego "I" can *never* and *will never* Awaken. There is absolutely nothing that you – as the body-mind – can do to go beyond yourself. Trying to surrender your attachments without actually surrendering the personal "I", is like cutting the leaves and branches off a tree without uprooting it. Until and unless we cut the root, the branches and leaves will grow back again. So the event of True Awakening occurs when the *presumption* of you – as the ego "I" – is exploded, vanished, sublimed. But YOU can't do THAT. Only That Which IS can "do" That! Only when your limited consciousness is absorbed into That Which Is does Awakening Awaken. The whirlpool cannot *become* the Ocean, it can only be undone through the recognition that it already *Is* the Ocean, and that Its True Nature has been water all along.

However, if we just passively choose to "do nothing" in a posture of defeat in response to this truth, if we settle for our habitual experience of life while vaguely hoping that Awakening might "accidentally" occur through Grace, then it is very unlikely that we will ever Awaken. Thus there is a Great Paradox at the heart of the Awakening Process. On the one hand, self-purifying activity, and even a prolonged regimen of disciplines, may help us to gradually release our energy and attention from the binding power of psychological patterning and material objects, and therefore make us more susceptible to Awakening. Yet on the other hand, it is also true that the event of Awakening Itself is uncaused in nature, and is more akin to a discontinuous leap than a result of a progressive path.

Because Awakening is a radical shift in perception that reveals a new order of Reality instantaneously there is no time-bound separate sense of "I" that can survive this transition. The ego "I" cannot get "there" from "here". It must be sacrificed in the Fire of the Heart. Therefore Awakening is not an attainment that "I" can add to "my" list of attainments, because the truth is that there is absolutely nothing to attain. Awakening is not an experience that "I" can add to "my" collection of experiences, because Awakening is not an experience that occurs in time. The limited dream character, that is the illusion of independent self-existence, wants to attain and possess the pot of gold at the end of the spiritual rainbow called Awakening or Enlightenment, but that "pot of gold" can only be discovered when the seeker dies.

*****

Awakening is the Greatest Wonder, Riddle, Paradox and "Aha!" moment because it operates outside of the matrix of time and space. From a time bound and spatially limited self-contracted consciousness we spontaneously find ourselves existing in and as boundless, unqualified Consciousness Itself, with no time having passed and no space having been traveled. Because the miracle of Awakening is not dependent on conditions, and is not caused by conditions, this radical insight and understanding is available at each and every moment; not only when we drop all activity and sit down to meditate.

If what I am saying is true then it means that the experience that you are already having right now of reading these words is *already It.* Your mind may immediately object by producing thoughts like, "How can *this* really be *It*? Isn't this the same consciousness that I have always been experiencing?" Ask yourself, "To which "I" do such thoughts refer?" Where did the "I" that is reading these words come from? Was it born along with your body? Will it be gone when you die? Listen for the ring of a deeper truth. So the answer to the question above is yes It *is* the same Consciousness (with a capital C) that you have always been experiencing. It is the prior I AM that has always been continuous and unchanging throughout all of the changes of inner and outer phenomena that have manifested as, what you call, "my" life, you just hadn't realized it yet!

The self-referential sense of "I", the "I" that appears as the psychological whirlpool and flesh-bound capsule of life that is the possessor of its ongoing drama called "my" life, can never know this Truth. The ego "I" by definition can only see the world, and all the sentient beings and phenomena that populate it, as intrinsically "other". But our most prior and most intimate experience of "I" makes no such distinctions.

*****

According to the Old Testament, God supposedly said to Moses, "I AM that I AM", and indeed "I" is the Holy Name, the Holy Word that is used by everyone in all languages more than any other word. Yet for the vast majority of human beings "I" refers exclusively to the psychophysical whirlpool of conditional historical existence. But when "I" Awaken from that dream of separateness, then who "I AM" is the self-authenticating beacon of Consciousness Itself, shining through a unique body-mind that illuminates the creative display of the world and universe.

When the illusory bubble of independent self-existence pops, then we realize that nothing can come into existence without Consciousness. Nothing can appear without the shining beacon of I AM giving itself utterly, intimately and entirely to that particular appearance. Therefore, when we Awaken to our True Self there is a wordless "YES" to the totality of Life, for there is the tacit recognition that, in some inconceivable way, we *are* the totality of Life. Whatever appears in our awareness appears in and as our True Self – the dimensionless field of pure sensitivity, receptivity and intelligence that is intimately one with every experience as a modification of its own Being.

Deeply resting at the heart of all experience, free to take the shape of all experience and yet independent of all experience, the pure immediacy of I AM forever shines forth. Awakening is essentially a recognition of the fact that we always already exist *in and as* that Being that always already transcends and includes everything. In Reality we were *never* separate, *never* limited and *never* unfree. Nothing that we could ever add, and nothing that we could ever do, to modify our experience, could possibly bring us any closer to who and what we already ARE. This radical understanding is an instantaneous process, an intelligent, happy process, not one of meditating on our own limitations, but a process of instantly transcending them in Reality. And as this understanding matures our experience of life becomes more and more full and ecstatic. We realize that the apparently separate "I" who needs to be fulfilled doesn't even exist to be destroyed!

*****

The mind cannot and will never be capable of comprehending this formless Presence that permeates all. The mind can know NOTHING of what Life and Consciousness *really* are. The mind must fall into the Heart. Then the mind is made usable and pliable, rather than persisting as a pattern that binds. The mind – that remarkable mechanism of attention, differentiation and deduction – is then freed to be a servant. Then it assumes its rightful place as a tool to assist us in navigating gracefully through this fleeting world of time and space, instead of it being our slave master endlessly embroiling us in the snares of attachment, narcissism and doubt.

Of course every way in which I or anyone attempts to describe Awakening in words is subject to the limitations of the language of our current level of consciousness that is based on the fundamental premise of duality, of "I" and "you" and "it". That is why the brightly burning flame of aspiration to be Free must be alive in our Hearts, that is why being oriented toward a radically open disposition of not knowing in relationship to the wonder of existence is so essential. That is why Jesus said, "Truly I tell you, unless you change and become like little children, you will never enter the kingdom of Heaven." For only if we become innocent, only if we are wide open and willing to let go and die to the known over and over again, will the glorious imminence of Awakening have room to dawn within us and potentially take root to such a degree that we, as individuated body-mind vehicles, will never be the same again.

# Chapter 18

# Wide Open Wonder

I would like to explore this whole matter of becoming innocent more deeply as it is another ever-present doorway into the discovery of our True Nature. Our deeply ingrained habitual tendency is to project conventions of familiarity and identification onto arising patterns of essentially unknown phenomena. This is how we make sense out of life. Of course a degree of familiarity is needed to function as a human being in this world, but by "making sense out of life" in this way we also tend to define it within the conditions of our past knowledge and experience. Then what is known and familiar to us becomes the definition and limitation of our experience of life. We move unthinkingly against a changing panorama, dragging along dead images of live moments from the past. We tend to eat, sleep, work and play like automatons, sleepwalking through life and spinning like tops. If we are habituated to simply coping with the conditions of life in this way, then our suffering makes us dull, and getting dull is one of the ways we cope with life. Then we are basically practicing a life of desensitizing ourselves to Reality, to the Divine Mystery. Trapped in the seeker's mind that desperately seeks a little consolation and pleasure wherever it can be found, we settle for grinding out our life while locked into our unquestioned presumptions.

One way to get a sense of how free or bound you are by the whirlpool of the ego "I" is to reflect on how often each day you allow the habit of familiarity to creep in? How often do you allow your intimate partner to get away with a quick peck on the cheek before they dart off to something very important like work while your love dies? And how often do you do the same? How often are you rushing ahead of yourself, your energy and attention stressfully focused on wanting to be "there" instead of being "here"? How often do you take your partner, your children, your parents, your pets, the blessings of your life, the warm glow of the sunshine and the beauty of the trees for granted?

In all these ways and in many others, that are no doubt coming to mind as you read this, we tend to become desensitized and locked into what feels familiar and secure to us. This is because that feels preferable to bearing the potential discomfort of what appears to be unfamiliar and unknown. Our attachment to what is known and familiar results in our compulsive repetition of that which is known and familiar, and so over time a momentum is created and we are not even aware anymore of how numb, closed and conditioned our relationship to life has become. But if we deeply inspect this moment *as it is*, free from the momentum of superimposition based on past knowledge and experience, we will realize that there is really nothing familiar or known about it.

Probably you have had glimpses of this. For example, have you ever looked at someone or something that is totally familiar to you and suddenly you have no sense whatsoever of who they are or what it is? In other words, you see the familiar form, but there is no "instant recall" based on past associations. You see the person, the tree, the landscape, or the apple *as it is* without any mental labeling of any kind. And in that seeing of the person or the object *as it is* there is an ineffable blessing of innocence, of what I like to call Wide Open Wonder.

I often experience this with my wife Cynthia, my closest companion in life. As we have been married for many years, and were close friends for many years before that, we know each other very, very well. However, because we are more interested in Freedom than in familiarity, in newness rather than repetition, we often surprise and challenge any normalcy in each other. While we know a lot about each other and live intimately together there is often a sense of not knowing who the other is that always comes with a vivid quality of wonder and amazement. In that not knowing there is no imposition of familiarity from the past, there is a tacit recognition of the One Mystery looking through our eyes and animating our lives together. So even if you are very familiar with someone based on past history and experience, even if you know all about them as an individual, when you come together in a context of Spiritual Awakening and Wide Open Wonder there is a spark of not knowing that comes to the foreground. And that spark is the space from which unqualified joy and freshness springs.

This is one of the reasons why so many people who are awakening spiritually long to come together with others who also share their passion for Freedom.  As we Awaken we feel more and more stifled by the presumption of familiarity that most people live in, and so we long for a context of relatedness in which True Freedom, True Love and Wide Open Wonder can be uninhibitedly expressed.  When we come together with others in a spirit of open exploration we may experience the surge of an ecstatic intimacy that emerges out of this ground of not knowing.  And in that ecstatic intimacy, while we may still be aware of all that we know about one another personally and historically, we directly experience that what we essentially *are* is unknown, is inherently mysterious.

Coming together in not knowing, in Wide Open Wonder, is thrilling because it is the lived experience of two or more individuals being overwhelmed by the One Unknowable Mystery that we all are.  Then the spiritual truth of non-separation, of Non-Duality or not-twoness, is experienced not only as a Revelation in which we perceive that everything "out there" is arising in and as our Conscious Presence, but it is also experienced as a literal manifestation of a transfigured humanity in relationship in time and space.  When this occurs a door opens to another dimension and a Love that infinitely transcends the personal dimension of existence, explodes into Being.  I will explore the nature and potential of this Freedom and Love that can emerge between awakening individuals later in this book.

*****

One way to understand how the Awakening Process begins is that it is when, for whatever reason, we make room inside ourselves for *not knowing* who we are, *not knowing* why we are here and *not knowing* what life is all about. Instead of settling for the security of quick and easy answers that have been handed down to us from family, our education and from society at large, or even from time-honoured spiritual traditions, we discover a willingness to live in and as the big questions themselves: Who am I? Why am I here? How shall I live? What is Life all about?

As soon as we open to these big questions without needing to grasp for an answer, innocent curiosity begins to shine forth. Wide Open Wonder begins to crack asunder the hard shell of our unexamined assumptions and beliefs, and even the very perceptual frameworks with which we create a world for ourselves to live in.

Ask yourself honestly: Do you think that you know who you are, why you are here and what life is all about? If you have sincerely opened your Heart to the content of the last few chapters I hope that there is a lot more room for what you do not know than there was previously. But if you recognize that you are usually quite sure that you know who you are and what life is all about, but you also confess that your life is simultaneously characterized by neurotic drama, habitual unhappiness, frustration and fear, then these are signs that you are hypnotized by unexamined assumptions that are keeping you in a self-contracted semi-conscious trance. I say, "trance", because when we feel secure in our apparent knowledge of who we are, why we are

here and what life is all about, we effectively anaesthetize ourselves
to the perpetually awesome wonder of existence. We live in a familiar
psychological bubble of habitual patterns and interpretations of life
that keep us estranged from the limitless mystery of Pure Existence.

# Chapter 19

# Ignorance Is Bliss

Henry David Thoreau famously said, "most men live lives of quiet desperation". Do you want to settle for a life of "quiet desperation", living in a consensus trance propelled by the Great Search, that shuts out the Wide Open Wonder of Pure Experiencing? Or do you want to venture beyond all fear, familiarity and knowing, revive your capacity for the unselfconscious innocence that you swam in as a child, and boldly take a journey into the ultimate Mystery of Existence?

A good place to start that journey in any given moment is by going straight to the unexamined presumption that underlies all human behaviour and is the root of all our knowing. That presumption is our experience of "I" that refers to a subjective inner self that thinks and feels and that initiates speech and actions.

The unexamined presumption that "I" am inside the body and "I" am the thought that initiates action concretizes our sense of being the subjective "I". From that point of subjectivity we relate to our body as a medium that exists between "I" and everything else that is outside the body. Thus, our habitual felt self-sense is that we are a continuity of psychological experience that is hidden within our breathing body, which is a fleshy wrapping around this life of the independent inner subject. But is this really so? Is the "I" really within?

If we don't inquire very deeply into our actual experience we tend to presume that thought precedes our speaking and activity. But it doesn't take much self-observation to realize that there are many times when we speak and act without thinking at all, and that also there are times when our speech and action co-arises with thinking. If we do not think a word before speaking it, then we could say that speech is identical to thought in that instance. Then thought *is* speech. They co-arise as one event. Then there are the times when we are silent and thought goes on, but does that mean that thought is distinct from speech or action? Perhaps it is only because we spend so much of our time dwelling upon the apparently "inward" permutations of thinking that we presume that there is a concrete independent subject behind thought and speech?

As I am writing this book sometimes "I" think and then "I" write. But when a flow begins to arise "I" often cease to think first and simply write. This is when writing is most enjoyable and creative. This is an example of what is often called a "flow state". Experiencing a flow state while writing is often called a "stream of consciousness", because the thinking mind is not the source of the writing. The thinking mind only reflects in retrospect on what has been written.

I am sure that you have had experiences of "flow states" such as this, when you give yourself completely to doing something that you love. It could be while playing music, dancing, doing sports, gardening, or making love to your beloved. Ask yourself why you love to do what you do. You will probably find that when you are propelled into that activity most fully you *lose* yourself. You *forget* yourself. When being and doing become one flow you are Happy! Life is simple and overwhelmingly gorgeous in its scintillating sweetness. You are without any independent subjectivity. You, whoever you are, are merged with the activity itself. Thought, in these instances, does not necessarily precede or accompany what is being done. The presumed separate, inner initiator of writing dissolves into writing itself. The dancer dissolves into the dance. The painter dissolves into the painting. The lover dissolves into the Beloved. So who or what, then, am "I"?

When being and doing become indistinguishable, when we merge with an activity – writing in my example – there is no perceivable separate, inner, thinking self that is the "doer". Then "I" appear to be mysterious and shapeless inside, writing without a center. Yet I clearly have not disappeared. There is still an "I" that is aware that "I" am writing. There is an "I" that witnesses the action of writing, even if there is no thought. "I" even witness the thought "I am writing". So the "I am writing" thought is perceived by a Witnessing I AM that is prior to the subjective concept of "I". This Witnessing I AM is utterly unknowable and indefinable, since it witnesses all but is Itself never witnessed. The thought "I", and every thought, sensation and experience arises within that indefinable I AM Presence. Even the manifest appearance of my hands typing on the keyboard, the desk underneath it, and the surrounding space of the room in which "I" am writing, and the cool breeze coming through the open door caressing my skin, is all arising in and is witnessed by, this indefinable I AM that cannot see or know itself as an object.

Therefore "I" think, or say that "I" think, but the thought "I" and all experiences ascribed to "I" are all witnessed or intuitively felt to arise within an I AM Presence that is not identified or known concretely in relationship to any other thing. The subjective, independent sense of "I" that we all presume to be "me", is no different from thinking itself, or speech or action itself, indeed it cannot be separated out from the entire arising field of manifest existence. Therefore, "I" is not inside the body. "I" co-arises with the whole process of the psychophysical being *and* all of its perceived surroundings. It is all one co-arising event.

I AM or Consciousness Itself is not found exclusively within or without. I AM or Consciousness Itself exists coincident with all arising conditions, subjective or objective simultaneously. Now isn't that a Wonder?

*****

After that brief magical mystery tour into the illusory and elusive nature of the subjective, inward "I", is it not obvious that the Truth is that we do *not* really know who we are, why we are here and what Life is all about, and that the mere fact of our existence is inherently mysterious? Think about it. Can you account for the appearance of your body here? I certainly cannot account for mine! Did you *do* your own birth? Are you breathing yourself, living yourself and creating yourself at this moment?

Consider that the primary way in which we reference our habitual sense of self is through the stream of thought. But what *is* thought really? Do we even know what a thought *is*? I can tell you that I have no idea. You and I are both somehow implicated, involved in thoughts, just as we are with our entire psychophysical experience, but do we know in actuality what a thought really *is* or how or why thought arises, or what this body *is* or how or why this body arises? Did we create this body and do we create our thoughts?

If we stop whatever we are doing for a few moments, and let everything be as it is, we will see that we *obviously* do not breathe our bodies and nor do we intentionally generate all of our thoughts. Of course, when we choose to apply our capacity for intentionality and will we can use the medium of thought (and the body) as a functional mechanism to navigate, to plan, to imagine, to create and to act. But so much of the mundane, chattering stuff of thought that we experience is completely beyond our conscious control or creation, just as is our dreaming at night and the physical processes of digestion and breathing.

My point in posing these questions is to illustrate how our adventure of existence is inherently mysterious and yet, for most human beings, the experience and knowledge of life is characterized by an embedded and deadening sense of familiarity. What seems to be mundane is in fact miraculous! What seems to be extra-ordinary is in fact extraordinary!

Obviously we depend on a certain degree of familiarity to function in the world and we might think that if everything became utterly unfamiliar to us then we would go insane. We might become so disorientated that we could not function coherently anymore. That might happen to some degree if we self-consciously tried to superimpose this disposition of not knowing upon ourselves, a strategy that I do not recommend. Rather what I am suggesting is that it is possible to Awaken to Wide Open Wonder even in the midst of the otherwise familiar conditions of existence.

When the mind as knowledge dissolves in not knowing, we see that we are not able to find out who we are. I have no idea who or what I am, and you cannot find out who or what you are either. "I" cannot step back and know "me" because "I" cannot observe "me" as an object. Thus, we see that there really is no inward "I". The "I" that we indicate as being "me" is only a functional convention of self-reference. It is a way for our individuated body-minds to organize experience in relation to themselves. That conventional self-reference called "I" can have all kinds of materialistic, scientific, and apparently rational notions about who "I" am, what Life is about and why "I" am here, or it can have all kinds of spiritual, mystical and philosophical notions about who "I" am, what Life is about and why "I" am here, but the ultimate fact staring us all in the face is that we truly have *no idea whatsoever!*

*****

In fact to know everything about anything – a peach, for example – would mean knowing everything about the entire universe, because everything is absolutely interrelated. As some truly progressive scientists are beginning to discover, we cannot separate ourselves from anything in order to know what it is. Every apparent thing is entangled with every other apparent thing. The physicists, who have discovered that the observer affects the observed, call this quantum entanglement. So even science, the great Western means of "making sense of everything" is discovering that no separate, discrete "things" actually exist. Every apparent thing, as Gautama Buddha said, is *dependently originated*, is inextricably intertwined with every other apparent thing.

When we truly let in the utter incredibleness of everything, we realize that we do not, and can never, know who we are, what life is, why we are here, or what any thing that arises – body, tree, flower, bird, moon, star or peach – actually *is. We do not even know why we are what we are!*

We can say and think for example that, "All is One" or "Everything is an expression of the Divine" or "God is Love", but in some more fundamental sense this is all complete nonsense. Spiritual concepts such as these enable us to somehow grasp and make the Mystery of our existence somewhat orderly, palatable and intelligible, but in Reality our conceptions do not amount to anything that we can hold onto. We tend to appeal to these kinds of images and concepts to console ourselves and to induce a feeling sense of living contact with Divinity, but can we be free of our need for the universe to make any sense whatsoever? We can attempt to make sense out of it in our fear, but if we are simply present to all that is arising and are willing to not know in the midst of it all, then we are not obliged to make sense out of it. Why? Because we are *already Happy!*

Nothing could seem more "crazy" than to be *already* Happy in this earthly realm, because there is no apparent justification for it. It is not *reasonable* to be Happy, let alone *already* Happy. On the contrary, if we thoroughly examine this world, and we really see what is happening here, there is very good reason to feel very unhappy. There is no philosophy based on our experience here that can make us Happy. Rather it is only the resort to Wide Open Wonder, to the ever-new recognition that Existence is *already* miraculous and therefore nothing fantastic has to happen, that allows us to be Happy.

\*\*\*\*\*

Now let us zoom out for a few moments and take an imaginary "God's Eye" view of our (so they say) pale blue dot spinning in this unfathomable universe. Gaze upon this planet populated by the burgeoning billions of the human race running here and there. They are busy making arrangements, intent on achieving this and that. They are ever proliferating more and more complexity and chaos, earnestly competing, fighting and struggling, wantonly destroying their own Mother Earth, and none of them have the slightest idea what is really going on. Trapped in the barbed-wire entanglement of their subjectivity, and the myopic allure of their evermore-sophisticated technological devices, oblivious to the motivating lie of separate existence and the billions of destinies that are its reaction, they blindly play out their script amongst endless probabilities.

From the point of view of "God's Eye" (which is not actually a "point" of view), all knowledge and all subjectivity, and the entire outward and inward adventure of all seeking selves, is absolutely unnecessary nonsense. Such a radical Revelation in which we behold both the utter absurdity of our condition and the inconceivable suffering that is its result, makes us laugh or cry or both. This is an interesting paradox to contemplate.

As disconcerting and even scary as this all may feel to let in, if we lean into this bottomless well of Mystery with Wide Open Wonder, what we will find is not a grim void of meaninglessness and despair as our ego "I" will fear, but the unmistakable thrill of the Unknown. We will stumble upon the ebullient Bright Shout of self-arising Happiness and Freedom. This happens because not knowing IS Freedom. The fact that you and I do not know *is IT*. Awakening is immediate release from the illusion of knowledge. All things arise and nothing is known. Nothing is known and everything happens. Every moment represents the death and creation of everything, all is born anew in every moment. Resting in that Wide Open Wonder is the source of all true wisdom. In fact, in the end it is true, as the saying goes, "Ignorance *is* Bliss."

*****

Think about it. You and I could get together and share all that we have experienced, all that we have known, seen and done, but does that really mean that we know anything conclusive about What Really

Matters? In all other fields of human endeavor we can say that the more we learn the more we know, and this is commonly understood as "knowledge". From that point of view the Unknown is simply that which we do not yet know. But when it comes to the core spiritual endeavor of human life, which is living inside the big questions like "Who am I?" and "Why am I here?", then the more that we do authentically come to know or understand, the more we are paradoxically divested of our accumulated knowledge. For the Unknown *is* unknowable, and it can only be *known* through direct intuition, not through the medium of mind. And it is this pure intuitive knowing of the Heart, that springs up from the ground of not knowing, that is the jubilant fountainhead of Freedom and Ecstasy.

All I can tell you is that when we stop *needing to know* we are Happy! Then we live every blessed day in wordless gratitude for this incredible, profound, mind-blowing, humbling Mystery that is a source of endless fascination and wonder. It is indeed Wonder-Full!

# Chapter 20

# The Secret of Freedom

BY NOW I have introduced you to two direct doorways into Spiritual Awakening – True Meditation and Wide Open Wonder. Both doorways open you to the same recognition of your True Nature, because when you let everything be as it is in True Meditation or abide in the disposition of Wide Open Wonder, you are aligning with the deepest dimension of your Self that is always already Free from the superimposition of separate existence.

This Being-Consciousness, Spirit, God, as we have been exploring, is synonymous with your most essential sense of I AM, the I AM that exists prior to everything that arises, whether in your normal waking state, in the dream state or in deep dreamless sleep. That primordial Consciousness or I AM Presence has never had a relationship to anything that ever happened in time, because it always abides prior to the world of time, form, and mind.

Under the right circumstances, like on a long meditation retreat for example, it is not difficult to have a powerful *experience* of Consciousness. By this I mean to experience ineffable Peace, Bliss, Emptiness, as all phenomenal objects, gross and subtle, organically fall away. When we give ourselves wholeheartedly to True Meditation practice over a long period of time in conducive conditions, we sink ever more deeply into that Consciousness, into that prior I AMness, which I likened earlier to sinking into the depths of the ocean.

In this metaphor the waves on the surface of the ocean represent our psychological experience, which is usually in the foreground and very apparent in our day-to-day lives where we have to think, engage and respond, and the bottom of the ocean represents that depth in which our experience of being a "psychological self" dissolves completely. In those moments when we sink to the bottom of the ocean, we realize that we are not, and never have been, limited and defined by the waves on the surface, but that we are the vastness of the entire ocean itself.

If we are serious in our aspiration to Awaken then it is very important to taste the inherent liberation of our own infinite depth. Going on a meditation retreat is a rare opportunity to relinquish outer distractions and obligations, and allow ourselves to sink ever more deeply into the infinite ocean of Consciousness below the waves of thought and emotion. However, as important and deeply inspiring as that kind of extended experience of Peace, Bliss and Silence can be, it will not necessarily, in and of itself, teach us how to have a liberated *relationship* to the chaos of our own mind and emotions when we are walking, talking and acting in the world.

Sinking into the depths of Pure Being-Consciousness, in the way that is possible on a meditation retreat for example, will always be profoundly affirming of the spiritual truth that who we are is not ultimately what we think or feel, or anything that we can know or perceive with the mind. If we go deep enough, consistently enough, we will realize that the sense of being a separate, limited, historical personality and skin-encapsulated ego "I" is quite simply an illusion. When we deeply recognize this we experience the Ecstasy of Freedom, in the true sense of that word "ex-static", meaning that we are no longer "stuck", no longer defined, no longer limited, and no longer "static".

As significant as such insights and experiences of Awakening can be, there is still the transformative challenge of integrating these revelations into our everyday life of embodied humanity in this world. As I wrote earlier, when we truly Awaken we recognize that "by habit we have been committed to the destiny of separation, suffering and delusion, and yet by Nature we are *already, and always have been, Unified, Happy and Free*." That is why if we want to *live* an Awakened Life it is equally important to learn how to have a liberated relationship to the chaos of emotions that may be raging on the surface of the ocean when a storm is passing through.

For most of us who are living an active and engaged life in the 21<sup>st</sup> century, the capacity to have a liberated relationship to the chaos of the human experience may ultimately be a source of greater confidence and freedom than the felt experience of infinite Depth, Peace and Ecstasy. The equanimity that I am pointing towards dawns when we begin to understand that, from the deepest perspective, being at the surface of the ocean amongst the choppy waves is no different from being at the bottom of the ocean, even if it doesn't necessarily *feel* that way. Only then can we fully integrate one of the most difficult things to grasp about the Awakening Process, which is that Spiritual Freedom *is not a feeling.*

Freedom is not any particular experience, no matter how profound the experience may be. Freedom transcends Peace; Freedom transcends Bliss; Freedom transcends Ecstasy. Peace, Bliss and Ecstasy are *qualities* of Consciousness that may emerge spontaneously in the disposition of Wide Open Wonder, or when we meditate for prolonged periods. When we experience these qualities we *feel* free, but that is a *feeling* of freedom, it is not necessarily *Freedom Itself.* We enjoy those subtle and inspiring deeper states and qualities of Consciousness as and when they arise, but if we are practicing True Meditation we will recognize that the inherent Freedom of Consciousness Itself transcends even our experience of these refined states and subtle feelings.

This is why someone can have an experience of sinking into the Peace, Bliss and Ecstasy of Consciousness and *feel* during that experience as if they are Free, but that does not mean that they are actually a deeply liberated human being in the context of their day to day life. And on the other hand, someone who *is* a deeply spiritually awakened human being may experience fear, confusion and intense pain at times, and not lose their rootedness in the knowing, before thought, of their essential Freedom despite the turbulence that they are experiencing.

The feeling quality of our experience will always be fluctuating, and the more so if we live a deeply engaged life in the world. So if we want to be a spiritually awakened human being, if we want to realize it, to *make it real*, then that Liberation is dependent only on the *relationship* we are having to our psychological experience, it is not dependent upon the quality or the content of experience itself.

So going back to our metaphor of the waves and the ocean, you will come to understand that whether you are resting in ecstatic Peace, Bliss and Ecstasy on the ocean floor, or whether you are navigating complex and challenging waves on the surface in your daily life, *it is all water*. Or, put another way, *it is all Consciousness*. You come to understand and realize that your psychological experience of thought and emotion, and indeed the entire world in which "you" apparently arise, is a modification of Consciousness just as the waves are a modification of the ocean. You are the ocean *and* the wave. You realize that Consciousness is not exclusive of the world of form, rather it pervades the entire realm of form, including the body-mind itself.

Once we deeply understand that the purpose of True Meditation, and by extension our Awakened Life, is to maintain a *posture* of Freedom *no matter what our inner experience may be*, then we cease to judge the quality of our meditation or our present life circumstance as "good" or "bad" based on our personal psychological experience and our preferences. In fact, we will recognize that sitting down to meditate when we are experiencing emotional chaos and confusion may be *more* significant than sitting down to meditate while experiencing a "quiet mind" or sublime states of bliss and ecstasy.

\*\*\*\*\*

Can we bear the battering of the waves when there is a storm raging without being deeply disturbed by any of it? Is it not true that if we cannot maintain our equilibrium while the storm is raging when we are sitting still in meditation, then there is simply no way that we will be able to bear it when we are walking and talking and acting in the world? So if we do not want others (usually those we love and care about the most) to inevitably suffer the consequences of our psychological turmoil, if we want to learn how to take responsibility for our mind and emotions, then we must resolve not to be victimized or intimidated by our psychological experience. Then we will understand that our spiritual practice is not only about experiencing Freedom from our psychological experience during the meditation session, it is also about potentially being so grounded in that Freedom that we will not create unnecessary suffering for ourselves or others in our everyday life.

We all have to be careful with the choices we make in relationship to our own psychological experience, because our actions always have consequences. Whenever we allow ourselves to react unconsciously to the inner storms of thought and emotion then we, and those close to us, will experience the result. As we Awaken more and more deeply to who we really are, we will perceive directly that Life and Consciousness is one unified Whole. We will begin to care about the impact that our individuated self-expression is having on the totality, because we perceive that everything that we do or say is sending out ripples and has a gross or subtle effect on that Whole.

When we let everything be as it is, regardless of whether we are having the most sublime, glorious, ecstatic experiences or frightening, dark, and malicious experiences and impulses, we remain fundamentally unmoved and present. That does not mean that we dissociate from or deny our experience, but that we *transcend and include* it in a larger embrace. We are at one with the *totality* of what is, regardless of the content of what is.

As we become more grounded in that essential unification with what is, when the storms come and pass and we recognize that we have not moved inwardly, we will experience a tremendous sense of Freedom, because we see and feel that our own aspiration to be Free is stronger than the chaos of our own mind. Seen in this way True Meditation literally becomes not only a door to the immediacy of Awakening here and now, but also a "training ground" for optimizing our capacity to respond creatively and compassionately to the inevitable challenges of living a committed life in this complex world of changes.

# Part V

# INTO THE FIRE

# Chapter 21

# Make It Real

Hopefully by this point in our shared journey, what I have endeavored to transmit to you has loosened up your habitual activity of self-contraction and self-identification. Through embracing the already liberated disposition of True Meditation and Wide Open Wonder, the potential to cut through the illusion of the ego "I" and its deadening fog of familiarity is ever-present.

Your deepest True Nature is, as I hope you have started to recognize by now, Pure Transcendent Consciousness which is *always already* radically Free from all phenomena high or low, pleasant or unpleasant. As you give yourself to the longing for Liberation, to the Fire of the Heart, to the disposition of Wide Open Wonder and the practice of True Meditation, you may be graced with piercing insights and ecstatic interludes of Awakened Consciousness. I call these kinds of insights and interludes Glimpses of Awakening. These Glimpses will give you a taste of Freedom, and deepen your faith in your capacity to become stabilized in this Awakened Consciousness. But as long as the patterning of the ego "I" is still your fundamental center of gravity, these Awakenings will continue to be Glimpses and most likely will not stick.

However, once we have irrevocably seen and consciously acknowledged that by Nature we are already Unified, Happy and Free *for real*, and we have reached a profound point of positive disillusionment with seeking and separation, then potentially a deep shift can occur at the core of our being. And with this shift we fundamentally come to the *end of all seeking*. We figuratively fall to our knees in humble recognition and surrender, for we now know unequivocally that we have found what we were looking for. Re-cognizing THAT, intuiting THAT, trusting in THAT, and being doubtless that THAT Absolute Reality is who we ultimately ARE *is* what Awakening IS. When we let go of seeking, we relinquish our fascination with higher states and even the authentic Glimpses of Awakening that we may have already had. Why? Because we have surrendered to the Truth that who we really are as Consciousness, Spirit, God, the Supreme Identity, is *Always Already The Case*.

While the living experiential immediacy of Freedom here and now will most likely fade from view as the momentum and veiling tendencies of the ego "I" intervene, if that penetration into our True Nature has been authentic and profound it burns an indelible imprint into our soul. By that I mean, come what may, we will never be able to completely forget it, because we now know that we have not only heard, but have literally *seen*, that there is nothing to attain and we are already Free, even if only for a searing instant.

When this occurs, in whichever way it occurs, whether spontaneously, or in the midst of True Meditation practice, or through the transmission of an Awakened Master, then we intuitively know it. What do we know? We know, beyond any doubt, that who we really ARE is not, and *never was*, the individual body-mind personality. Once we have directly seen and consciously acknowledged THAT, then *potentially*, from that moment on, we know that Awakening is not limited to, or defined by, any particular insight or experience, and that it is always available, and therefore is always a possibility in any moment. And we will also know, assuming we possess some humility and a realistic self-concept, that there is a tremendous momentum of conditioning or karma, as it is called in the East, that we need to take responsibility for if we are going to Realize – meaning to *make real* – our Awakening as a walking, talking individual in this world of time and space.

When our center of gravity shifts from seeking to finding, from the search to surrender, *everything* opens up. Our experience of life becomes full and deep and mysterious. There is a profound release of existential tension. We do not need to be convinced anymore, and as a result we discover a profound mind-transcending trust, both in ourselves as individuals and in Life itself. Having let go of all known reference points, we are in free-fall, as if we have jumped off a cliff without any need or desire to land anywhere.

This shift is the true beginning of the Awakening Process for only then can our energy and attention be fundamentally liberated from *seeking* for Truth to *surrendering* to Truth. Only through the radical discovery of our True Identity as Transcendent Being can we then fully engage the evolutionary call to Transformation.

*****

Truly becoming a finder in this sense is a pivotal shift that signals a sea change in the entire orientation of our individual life. If this shift has authentically occurred it means that the revelation of Awakening has penetrated the deepest levels of our psyche. The clamor and complexity of the ego "I" has subsided sufficiently to reveal a stark absolute simplicity. In that simplicity there is the recognition that our present essential Happiness and Freedom is ultimately a matter of choice. We recognize and humbly acknowledge that there are fundamentally only two movements that we can give ourselves to in any given moment, regardless of what is arising in the field of our experience. Either we contract in the midst of what arises, or we release. Either we choose to perpetuate the destiny of seeking and separation by holding onto the form of the whirlpool, or we surrender and abandon ourselves to the ocean. Either we are turning in upon a deadly illusion of a false and separate sense of self, or we are turned out and dissolved into unmitigated communion with Life, with Reality, with Consciousness Itself arising as the appearance of this world and its field of relations. There is nothing else. When we deeply see, acknowledge and accept this stark truth we are converted at the core of our Being. Then our orientation to our presence here on Earth is one of conversion from the self-serving agenda of "my" life, to the self-sacrificing surrender of the Fire of the Heart.

When we sincerely want to offer all that we are to God, to the Divine Principle, when we trust so deeply that we are willing to let go of personal control and give our life over to the very Consciousness that animates and encompasses all, then the Awakening Process begins in earnest.

# Chapter 22

# The Power That Knows The Way

Making it Real obviously implies that we will change in profound ways, but how does this process of Transformation occur?

One of the most common questions that I get asked when I am teaching is, "How am I going to change if I just let everything be as it is?" People worry that if they allow themselves to let go at the deepest levels of their being then they are going to become completely passive, and they will therefore not be motivated to change themselves, or make any significant contribution to the betterment of the world. I always respond by saying something like, "Don't worry you will not become an enlightened vegetable! Only when you are willing to let everything be as it is are you truly available for *real* change."

Usually our efforts to change ourselves issue from the subjective ground of the inward "I" which, as we have already discovered, is based on the unexamined presumption of something already being wrong, problematic or missing. Therefore, our efforts toward change are almost always stuck in the reactive paradigm of struggling *against* the way things are through some form of self-conscious willful effort or behaviour modification. In other words we are *trying* to do or not do something.

If we are very determined and disciplined such strategies of action can result in relative changes in our character, but it is still the ego "I" with its presumption of problematic limitation that is making the effort by redirecting attention, or by giving up this and choosing to do that. And so we effectively end up becoming a "new improved" version of who we already were.

While that path of "self-improvement" is obviously preferable to remaining an unimproved version of ourselves, if we are interested in authentic spiritual transformation, we have to go beyond this modality of *trying* to transcend ourselves. We have to recognize that we cannot change the deeper structures of our psychological conditioning through the act of self-directed will. And of course this puts us in a double bind, exactly the same double bind that we confront in the practice of True Meditation, namely that the Awakening Process requires us to transcend the motivational structure of the ego "I". But, of course, the ego "I" *cannot transcend itself*, so what are we to do...or not do?

The only way to discover the answer to that question is to have mind-transcending trust in the Fire of the Heart or, what I also like to call, the Power That Knows The Way, which is the guiding Light that issues from that Heart.

Through letting everything be as it is over and over and over again, we come to rest in the intuition of limitless, formless, ever-present,

Transcendent Being. Being does not do anything to itself, it simply IS. When we deeply recognize that our True Nature does not divide itself, such that one part does something to another part of itself, we see and deeply feel that to take the position of doing anything to ourselves in order to change ourselves contradicts our True Nature. When we recognize that contradiction, we see the futility of our usual sense of doing.

Thus the reactive tendency of the ego "I" is undermined by *first* radically accepting ourselves in all our imperfection, as we actually *are* in this very moment, and by radically accepting life as it is presented to us *right now* in all its potential complexity and pleasurable or painful circumstance. Only then will we be capable of transcending the reactive cycles of denial, avoidance and frustration. Only then will we be able to liberate ourselves from the embedded presumption of a problem, and make ourselves available to that Mystery that we have already intuited to be the very Heart and Ground of existence.

Resting in that disposition of faith, trust and surrender, we let go of all sense of dilemma, of all attachment to being somebody in particular and, most importantly, of *needing to know how to change*. We are freed to simply be present to the psychological pattern, or apparent obstacle, or life situation, that is presenting itself to us in this moment from an open, problem-free disposition of *not knowing* and *non-doing*.

Then, *and only then*, does the Power That Knows The Way spring organically out of this ground of not knowing and non-doing in the form of liberated intelligence, sensitivity and action. This liberated intelligence is *awake*, is interested, is curious, and is *available*. We are letting our experience be *as it is*, which is a *non-doing*, and simultaneously we are in a disposition of inquiry, carried on the wings of the Power That Knows The Way. We are simply being and from there we *allow* our doing to arise. It is a posture of *not knowing* and simultaneously *wanting to know* what's next?

It is through this dynamic interpenetration and harmonization of apparent opposites that the alchemy of the Awakening Process occurs. Letting everything be as it is is the passive, yielding pole of the Awakening Process. It relaxes the self-contraction and opens us up to the infusion of boundless Being that transcends and includes our locus of individuality. And the Power That Knows The Way, in the form of liberated feeling-intelligence, is the creative, agented pole, that is the expression of our individual conscious participation in the Process.

The way it works is that the more we meditate, the more we surrender to the truth of our prior Freedom and essential Happiness, the more our spontaneous participation in life becomes one of consistent, vibrant inquiry. The inquiry I am describing here is not predominantly mental. It doesn't mean that we are always sitting around thinking or always asking ourselves questions. It is not a self-willed analytical process of trying to be aware or trying to figure anything out. Rather from a ground of Wide Open Wonder, we spontaneously find ourselves more and more engaged in the natural observation, understanding and transcendence of the patterns and situations that bind.

The Power That Knows The Way is the natural and spontaneous flow of our interest in life. It is *living* Being pushing forth through the aperture of our individuality. And through this consistent flow of interest and curiosity our experience of life becomes increasingly direct, vivid and creatively simple.

Embracing the disposition of True Meditation we open to the immediacy of ever-present Being, and then the Power That Knows The Way, that is the impulse of a dynamic coming-to-Be, or Be-coming, spontaneously emerges. This impulse, this ability to respond creatively to life is not *our* "separate self" doing – it is Consciousness Itself manifesting in and through our surrendered body-mind. This is why it is so important that we approach True Meditation not only as a sitting practice, but also as an Awakened disposition that can potentially permeate our life as a walking, talking individual in this world. If we insist on being fixated in our meditative stillness, if we are strategically biased toward a detached exclusive abidance in the passive pole of Being, then we will inhibit the emergence of the Power That Knows The Way. That Power is the creative impulse of Consciousness Itself that is not only content to eternally BE but also "wants" to passionately BE-COME. Become what? Become an ever more radically free, creative and integrated expression of the Great One *in this world of time and space.*

When we yield to the Power That Knows The Way one could say that we become Divine Lovers. True Lovers do not fear dissolution, rather they live in surrendered submission to the Awakening Process.

True Lovers offer their body-minds in ecstatic awe at the sheer Wonder and Mystery of Existence, and through sacrificing themselves to this Love the secret purposes of the universe are fulfilled.

When we sit down to meditate, or simply allow ourselves to come to rest in those periods when we are inactive, we *lean back* into the passive, static pole of True Meditation. Then, when we reengage with life and the field of relations from a ground of unbroken trust, we *lean in* to the active, dynamic pole – the Power That Knows The Way – that spontaneously springs forth and carries us forward organically from that meditative ground of non-doing.

The passive pole practice – letting everything be as it is – is our openness to the *Revelation* of Awakened Consciousness here and now. The active pole practice – liberated feeling-intelligence in the form of inquiry and participatory love – is a natural expression of our taking responsibility for the *Realization* of our Awakening as a human being. To the degree that we sincerely aspire to be Free in every moment the Power That Knows The Way compels us to remain awake and vigilant, because we don't want to get sucked into the centrifugal force of the whirlpool of the ego "I", and also because, most importantly, we want to stay open to Being, to Be-coming, to Grace, to Mystery and to Love.

# Chapter 23

# The Divine Test

MAKING our Awakening *real* means undergoing the purifying ordeal of what I call the Divine Test. I like to use the word "Di-vine" to refer to the two "vines" or poles of the One Ultimate Reality. These poles are, as I have already been describing, the passive, receptive and static Being pole, associated with Shiva in Hindu Vedanta, and the active, dynamic Becoming pole, associated with Shakti. Another way to language this is that there is the Transcendent or *unmanifest* "vine" or pole and the Immanent or *manifest* "vine" or pole. We are all expressions of the One *Transcendent*, Eternal, Impersonal Being, that is radically Free, untouched and unaffected by all that arises and passes away, *and* simultaneously we are *Immanent* here on Earth as unique embodied individuals on a Great Adventure of evolutionary unfolding.

When we begin to authentically Awaken from the illusory dream of separate existence we are graced by the discovery of the radical immediacy of Being that is always already full, boundless and complete here and now. And that Awakening, if it is profound, catalyzes and fuels the Creative Process of our individual transformation in time and space. Hence, to truly live an Awakened Life, is to animate the Great Paradox in which we are simultaneously uncreated and created, unmoving and moving, both already timelessly at home and propelled into a remarkable human journey in this world of changes. As integral philosopher Ken Wilber succinctly puts it, we are both Waking Up and Growing Up simultaneously.

The Awakening Process is the dynamic Self-Realization that occurs when both of these poles or "vines" are fully activated and embraced. The Di-vine Test then, is the alchemy through which our individuality is gradually purified of the motivations and patterning of the self-contraction of the ego "I". And coincident with that process of purification, our individual self-expression progressively develops into a sensitive, discerning and creative organ of the True Self realizing Itself in time and space.

The alchemy of the Divine Test generates creative friction. This friction or "tapas", as it is called in India, is the inner "heat" that is felt, and must be endured, when the patterns that bind are being exposed and penetrated by the Light of discriminating wisdom. Igniting this alchemy is like stepping into a Fire – the Fire of the Heart. Once in the Fire, some slices of our conditioning may fall away organically without us even noticing or with very little effort, because they have already been seen through and rendered obsolete by the Light of observation and understanding. We might notice one day that a particular thought pattern, self-image or attachment has simply ceased to captivate our attention or has disappeared without us apparently doing anything. However, burning through the deeper embedded patterns that define our self-identity is another matter altogether, and this is where the Divine Test demands great courage and a willingness to endure tremendous heat and friction.

It is one thing to get to the point where we willingly step into the Fire, but it is quite another thing altogether to actually stay in the Fire when it is getting really hot! This is the most challenging part of the Awakening Process, and I can guarantee that you *will* want to run away from its flames when you have to confront something about yourself, or your life situation, that you cannot bear to face and are not yet willing to relinquish.

The Awakening Process demands that we *hold onto nothing*, that we let go of our strategies and our control. The Process is always propelling us in the direction of a "mountain peak" that at times ascends so steeply that we cannot find a foothold in it. The mountain peak looms in the rarified atmosphere of the Invisible, and therefore cannot sustain anything but that which is, or has become, Itself. Thus, the ego belongs to the climber's gear that must be jettisoned in the course of the ascent. And because this ascent demands more "resources" from us than we think we possess, we have to dig deep into the well of Consciousness in order to stay in the Fire of the Heart. Through consistent trust, faith and surrender, through all the trials and crises, we bring forth the creative intelligence of the Power That Knows The Way. And that Power purifies and transfigures our body-mind vehicle so that it may become a willing instrument of the Divine. Just as the mutating caterpillar cannot see or know the butterfly that it longs to become, so the awakening human being must surrender to the Power That Knows The Way to truly actualize his or her enlightened potential.

*****

The embedded patterning of our self-identity necessitates a pruning and a burning, and this is a painful and usually protracted ordeal. When we surrender in the way I have described, when we are willing to be raw and ragged in our vulnerability, when we are willing to bear the messiness that almost always accompanies the deep transformational alchemy of the Divine Test, then somehow, at some point, real change happens, sometimes inexplicably, out of the blue. This is when we experience the benediction of what is often described in the spiritual traditions as Grace. It is when the Mystery unmistakably takes over and we have the unequivocal experience of "Thy Will, not my will be done".

When we confront the Divine Tests the friction or "heat" occurs because we are afraid of our own dissolution. We do not want to let go of our known reference points for being who we are. We recoil in self-defense, and then the veiling power of the inward turning whirlpool makes it appear as if the ocean has disappeared, as if the Light has gone out. At times like this we may no longer be able to access any felt sense of inspiration for the Awakening Process. We may be overwhelmed by debilitating inertia, or paralyzing fear, or corrosive doubt, or rigid pride, or rebellious anger. The resources required to keep leaning in and to persevere do not seem to be available to us.

The Christian mystic St. John of the Cross, named this disconcerting and seemingly unendurable rite of passage "The Dark Night of the Soul". And of course the challenge is to metaphorically keep walking through the Dark Night while remaining open to God – to our intuited Transcendent Self – in a disposition of faith, trust and surrender until the Light begins to dawn once more.

Enduring the Dark Night is the Divine Test at its most challenging. At times we will falter, and we may fall down into the ego's whirlpool of doubt and fear, but if the Fire of the Heart is burning bright we will find the courage and perseverance to get back up, dust ourselves off, and keep walking through the darkness. If we are truly sincere we know that even if we falter, even if we fall and appear to be temporarily lost, we cannot turn away from the Awakening Process. We cannot remain ignorant and trapped in the cycle of conditional existence for that is simply not an option for us. The Fire that is burning in our Heart will not allow it. After stepping into the Fire and pulling back, and then stepping back in and then pulling back, and stepping back in, at some point we will come to a reckoning with whatever pattern or habit we are confronting. For example we will recognize that we absolutely do not want to be a selfish person anymore, or a victimized person anymore, or an aggressive person anymore. We sincerely want to stop lying, deceiving others and ourselves. We no longer want to be someone who is habitually self-indulgent, weak and afraid of a clear, straight and strong relationship to life. Whatever it is, we finally, deeply and genuinely, *want to be Free* of the habitual pattern that the Fire of the Heart is presenting to us, *more than we want anything else.*

Deep commitment, faith, trust and surrender give us the strength of character to keep going through all the stormy disorienting challenges of confronting our unconsciousness. Then, sooner or later, a shift in our character suddenly or gradually reveals itself. We may spontaneously find ourselves expressing more love, compassion, clarity and sensitivity. Or, if the issue has to do with some kind of addictive, enervating behavior, we simply stop smoking, or stop indulging in our degenerative habits. The conflicted push and pull of desire, guilt, sorrow, anger and reaction that was giving sustenance to our dilemma simply dissolves.

It happens this way because real change or transformation, as opposed to some form of self-conscious and willful behaviour modification, is not a matter of trying to do something or trying to not do something. It is a matter of doing something else that arises from that mysterious "no-place" that transcends all pairs of opposites – *something new* that is essentially free, and truly fulfilling. But that "something new" can only spring from a disposition of heartfelt surrender to the Mystery that calls us forward. This is why consistently practicing True Meditation, *especially* when we are navigating the Divine Tests, makes us more available to Grace, and progressively frees us from the necessity of always having to go through arduous trials of trying and then failing, trying and then failing, until we finally give up.

\*\*\*\*\*

Transformation literally means "transcending form". The ego "I" cannot "transcend form" because it is itself an activity of identification with form whether mental, emotional, or material. The ego may *try* to transform, to mimic its projected ideal of spiritual enlightenment, and to pretend by manipulating the apparatus of the body-mind. It may earnestly practice various techniques and focus attention on this chakra or that mantra. It may read, read and read all the spiritual classics. It may think, think, and think all the noble and "politically correct" spiritual notions. It may endeavor to behave in all the spiritually "politically correct" ways, and still its dominion over our individual self-expression will be intact.

True surrender to the Principle of Consciousness, of God, of Light, cannot be mimicked, cannot be approximated, cannot be "done", for when the ego "I" is truly surrendered it is unmistakable. You will recognize it in yourself and others as liberated, unselfconscious, spontaneous authenticity that carries the undeniable ring of Truth. That authentic response "transcends all form" in the sense that it is expressed by us as an individual, and yet we are simultaneously aware that we, as an individual body-mind, are *not the doer*. When the psychic mechanism of the ego "I" is transcended, our individual body-mind aligns with the Power That Knows The Way, and becomes a conduit for enlightened action.

However, by "spontaneous" I do not mean to suggest that the "doing" of enlightened action is always effortless. Far from it! Sometimes the tenacity and pressure of our psychological patterning, and the challenge of demanding situations and circumstances, will require us to make effort, and at times even tremendous effort. However, in those instances the making of the effort is itself spontaneous in the sense that there is a choicelessness about it. There is no fundamental doubt at the core of our being. So while resistance in the form of fear or pride may arise, there is no hesitation in us. We can cleanly cut through and beyond that resistance, and so be an expression of grace under pressure. Then the effort, the living force of action, is not coming from a conflicted or self-serving motivation, it is coming from an already unified motivation. Then the "I" of our self-reference is not the "I" doing the doing, Consciousness is.

Through being grounded in letting everything be as it is, in the disposition of True Meditation moment to moment, we progressively undermine the momentum of the ego's conflicted tendency. As we face whatever is arising with openness, curiosity and vulnerability, whether it is an "inward" matter of psychological content, or an "outward" matter of a life situation that is demanding a response, the self-contraction is yielded and the Light comes streaming in, and then out through our action.

This happens because we make ourselves *available*, because we *care* about responding authentically. The ego "I" only cares about *itself*. The True Self expressed as the Power That Knows The Way *cares*. And as we trust the Fire of the Heart evermore deeply, and allow this care to manifest, we will be astonished to discover over and over again that we have a profound and creative ability to respond to life that we never knew was there. We will observe ourselves more consistently and fearlessly taking responsibility for the truth that we know in our Heart, regardless of the consequences. We will observe in the midst of such action that our tendencies toward negativity, reactivity, and narcissism are being suddenly or gradually purified. We will witness our character becoming straightened, brightened, and emptied of self-serving motives. We will shift from fundamentally being a taker in relationship to life to being a *Giver*. And we will delight in the simple sweet joy of not needing to know who we are to authentically *be who we are*.

# Chapter 24

# Feeling the Heat

As should be clear at this stage of our journey, we are not primarily suffering from what is happening to us, we are suffering from what we are actually doing by tendency. We suffer because of our tendency to be addicted to feeling less than Love, less than Happy, less than Free. We tend to be hypnotized by movements of attention toward states that deplete us of energy and confine us to a life of mediocrity.

Because of this habitual condition of limitation the biggest motivating factor in our lives is that we all want to experience the relief and release of *feeling better*. But because we pursue feeling better in the context of the first or second Great Searches, that pursuit sooner or later ends in dissatisfaction and the seeking for repetition of fleeting earthly or heavenly highs. We might feel better periodically but we don't feel better as an *enduring* condition.

To *truly* feel better consistently in the deepest sense, we must learn to *feel* better, whatever we may be experiencing. And the only way we can learn to *feel* better, *feel* happy, *feel* love, and *feel* bliss, more and more consistently, is to divest ourselves of the clenched, deadening, loveless grip of our suffering inner "I" in each and every moment. That is the Divine Test that confronts us every single day.

When we start feeling the heat of the purifying fire and creative friction generated by the Divine Test, we automatically tend to withdraw. We usually quickly draw the conclusion that something is wrong, or that the heat should not be quite so hot, or even that this heat should not be happening at all! But as we grow in maturity in the Awakening Process, we begin to welcome the fact that the heat does not necessarily feel good and that its appearance does not conform to our preferences. Why? Because we trust in the Process and we know that we are coming up against the grain of our ingrained habits and tendencies. We cannot be victimized because we know that this heat is a result of our own action, of our own aspiration to be Free, of our own surrender to the Fire of the Heart. Feeling the heat is not just randomly happening to us, it is all part of the Divine Design.

The willing embrace of the heat becomes possible when we understand that the fact that we are feeling the heat does not mean that we have lost or are losing our Freedom. On the contrary, once we have deeply understood that Freedom is not a feeling, as I explained in the chapter "The Secret of Freedom", we understand that Freedom is essentially lived and demonstrated in how we *are* and what we *express*, not in how we feel or in what we think from one moment to the next. Then we experience the heat as a purifying fire. It is challenging, it is difficult and it is hot! It works against our embedded habits, constricted energies, unconscious impulses and adaptations. It frustrates and confounds them. However, if we are mature in our spiritual aspiration we do not complain, because we know that this is exactly what it takes to burn through our ignorance.

If we are continually monitoring the feeling quality of our experience to know how we are doing, then we will be continually modifying our commitment to the Divine Test based on our own subjective interpretation. We will *never* truly change that way. We must change our outward, objective action *first*, and then the inward, subjective dimension of our experience will change gradually over time. Usually spiritual seekers are *waiting* for their "insides" to change first, and this is why they remain spiritual *seekers*. The truth is that our subjective "insides" are the *last* to change. Our action must change *first*. Then the "inner" being will eventually reflect the new, rather than the old, adaptation. If we want to *feel* Free on the *inside* before we are willing to *act* Free on the *outside*, then we are *waiting*, we are postponing, we are bargaining with God, we are in a disposition of denial of Love and we are actively resisting the call of the Fire of the Heart.

What experience do we need to evolve? The one that we are having right now. In other words, The Way is what is *in the way*! If we try to bypass or avoid what is in the way *right now*. We will not burn through to the other side *right now*, we will be avoiding relationship with *what is*. But if we stay with *what is* right now, even if we feel absolutely terrible, we can still pass the Divine Test.

If we do not complain about the heat and allow it to be as it is, then the heat will cook us and eventually cool down. When there is little or nothing left to burn and our tendencies turn to ash, then we experience the coolness of equanimity. The Heat then transmutes into Light and we will *feel* the radiant current of Love-Bliss more continuously. But to the degree that we resist we *will* still feel the Heat, and so the challenge of the Divine Test is to submit to the purifying Fire of the Heart regardless of how it feels.

# Chapter 25

# Fake It Until You Make It

Once when I was explaining the principle that "your action must change first" to a gathering of students, one of them told me about an Indian Yogi who used the slang English phrase, "Fake it until you make it" to illustrate the same point. And that is an interesting and illuminating way to look at this, because of course from the point of view of the ego "I", acting in a way that goes contrary to how you actually feel does make you *feel* like you are pretending or faking it.

Imagine for example that you are feeling intensely jealous and competitive with someone because they have something that you wish you could have. But because you clearly see that this jealousy is a ridiculously egotistical movement, you *choose* to express sympathetic joy instead. Now in such an instance, if your attention is on *how you feel* – meaning that you take your psychological experience to be who you are – you may make an attempt to express sympathetic joy, but you will still feel yourself to be a fake. You will feel like you are pretending because you identify yourself as the subjective "I", looking from the *inside out.* Your primary focus is still on your *"insides"*, on how *"I"* *feel.* But if your attention is freed from the centrifugal force of the whirlpool, and encompasses the context of the other person and the whole situation, then you experience yourself as an expanded, non-localized *"I"*. Now your perspective is from the *outside in*, meaning that what is real to you is how you *objectively* are and what you *objectively* express, not how you *subjectively* feel. Then you do not feel like you are faking it at all, because what is *real* is how the other sees and experiences you, and not how you feel.

When you act in accordance with the truth of Prior Unity, regardless of what your "insides" may be telling you, then that egoistical pattern is *burned*, because not only did you *not* act upon it, you acted *contrary* to it. Then afterwards you may well *feel* great, but not because you actually felt good at the time, but because you have proven, through your own surrendered intention to be Free, that what you felt on the inside was *unreal.* And so the next time that you are in a situation that triggers that same reaction, you will potentially see it for what it is much more quickly, and you will not give your attention and energy to feeding that feeling, pattern or idea. In this way the binding power of the conditioned emotional pattern or idea becomes obsolete over time. This is *Liberation in action.*

*****

When we truly embrace the principle that *our action must change first*, then we will realize that our ego patterning is not hidden in an obscure network of internal psychological soup. Our ego "I" is right there to see in what we do every day. What we do, not what we say or what we think, points directly to the psychological roots of our dramatization. There is really no mystery about it, *if* we are willing to look.

Sometimes when people get interested in spiritual life and share that interest with others, what they are engaged in amounts to little more than a spiritualized form of psychotherapy in which they are endlessly sitting around talking about their neurosis, believing that this earnest process of introspection will expose the psychological roots of their suffering. But if we are sincerely interested in Awakening to our True Nature beyond the psychological self, then we will become less and less fascinated by the stories and complexities of our subjective experience and far more interested in observing what we actually do. As we become more interested in what we are actually doing and the effect of our actions on others, our dramatization of the self-contraction of ego becomes more obvious to us in real time, even in the small details of our behaviour.

As our commitment to the Awakening Process matures in this way, we will find that we do progressively *feel better* in the truest and deepest sense, regardless of what is happening. The backdrop or gestalt of the ego – the embedded sense that something is fundamentally wrong or missing – is gradually outshined by an enduring Happiness, Equanimity and Lightness of Being. We feel deeply infused with an increased sensitivity and capacity to love, not necessarily because we literally *feel good* all the time, but because we are living in and as our native fullness as an Awakening human being.

As we discover and actualize this deep joy, equilibrium and radiance more and more consistently throughout the ups and downs of life, we will come to understand and embody the principle of Light. But that "Light", or Lightness of Being, is now not only experienced in Glimpses of Awakening, in which the waves of mind and emotion are dispelled, as it was before. That Light is not a kind of giddy high or some kind of exaggerated bliss state. That Light is the "product" of consistently passing the Divine Test. That Light is clear, consistent and serene. It is not a matter of having a particular experience; it is a matter of the *transcendence* of experience. Our illusions and delusions are progressively burned up and then that Heat becomes Light. It *feels* like a Fire to the degree that our attention is wedded to those illusions and delusions, and at times the burning can be excruciating. But nonetheless, when we have the courage to endure the burning, we emerge Humorous, Happy and Full. Then we are a Force of Light to be reckoned with!

# Chapter 26

# Humility Heals

TRANSFORMATIONAL breakthroughs are made in the Awakening Process when we take full responsibility for the ego "I" as our own activity. When we unflinchingly face into our self-centered orientation to life, we allow ourselves to deeply feel the impact of our unconsciousness both on ourselves and on others. Facing into all aspects of our experience consistently in this way is a very humbling endeavor. Through truly facing into our habitual patterns, we allow them and ourselves to be exposed to the Light of Consciousness without withdrawing and hardening into moods of fear, anger, sorrow, resentment, or righteous indignation. The reactive tendency to avoid, to defend ourselves and to blame the other or circumstances may arise, but as we submit to the Awakening Process, we will learn how to gently and compassionately catch ourselves and to not dramatize these reactions.

Of course there will be many times that we do not catch ourselves and we will act out our conditioned patterning, but if our aspiration is sincere then our humility will deepen and we will develop a greater capacity to bear the searing burn of remorse as we confront our conceit, selfishness and lack of love. In this humility and raw vulnerability that feels so very naked and insecure, we will discover a great strength. It is the strength to bear the burning away of what is false and to stay with the ambiguity and uncertainty of the present moment. Being willing to bear the intensity of this kind of exposure opens our Heart and emboldens us to be accountable for our actions. And as we authentically do this, the remorse and shame naturally falls away and we move on, chastened and humbled by the purifying Fire of the Heart.

Humility is the cleansing, healing balm that comes after going through the Fire and staying true. Humility is our willingness to *lose face*, to put down our weapons, and to have our false self-images, our pride, our strategies of avoidance, burned clean in the Fire of the Heart. Humility is the strength to face our imperfection *without taking it personally*. True maturity begins in spiritual life with the capacity to sense and admit to our own craziness. Indeed, if we are not regularly embarrassed by how we are, we probably have not yet stepped into the Fire for real!

This maturity brings straightness, dignity, vulnerability, and also humour, that washes us clean and roots us in our prior Ground of Being. Humility, along with courage, is the most precious virtue on the spiritual path, and it is a virtue that we must consistently cultivate, because it usually does not come naturally to us. Humility alone undermines our pride, and realigns and restores us to our essential purity, goodness and native brightness through all the Divine Tests.

Every time that we go through a crisis of confrontation with the ego "I", and are then restored to the always already Free Ground of Being, we have a little more appreciation for the enormity of the ordeal of Transformation, and the fact that our, and everyone else's, egotistical patterns and habits are not essentially wrong. Rather we recognize that they are simply tendencies that persist because they have not yet been transmuted by the crisis of the Awakening Process. Every moment of crisis and regenerative growth is then seen and felt as a new beginning. And with every new beginning, and with an open and broken Heart, infused with newly replenished reservoirs of trust, courage and humility, we then turn once more toward the call of the Power That Knows The Way that beckons us forward, the next step revealing itself organically as we walk.

# Chapter 27

# Light on Shadow

In THE early stages of the Awakening Process we feel the suffering of our born existence much more acutely, because we can no longer engage in all the ordinary things that people do to distract themselves from that suffering. We can no longer blithely avoid confronting the suffering that underlies ordinary life by indulging obsessively in money, career, food, sex and casual entertainments. And so we are inevitably turned back on our suffering with much greater intensity.

As our habitual patterns and tendencies are progressively burned up in the purifying Fire of the Heart, the regenerative qualities of the Power That Knows The Way begin to emerge, but a very big part of that journey, especially in the initial stages, will most likely be an intensification of the energy of our neurosis. We may experience expansive states of peace and joy as we open into greater liberating depth, but then usually the "honeymoon" period eventually gives way to the backlash of the ego "I", as we are tempted once more to re-identify with our habitual patterning through various strategies of doubt, fear and pride.

In the midst of such an "ego backlash" we may feel that "I have lost it". But this is when our faith, trust and surrender are being tested, for how can we lose That which we *always already* are? Rather what occurs is that our identification with the whirlpool of ego acts like a veil that intervenes and *seems* to cut us off from the oceanic depth of our True Self. This veiling movement happens to the degree that there are remnants of attachment, resistance, confusion and impure motivation active in our psychophysical system. And that veil is seen through, and revealed to be an insubstantial superimposition of our own mind and emotions when, through our aspiration for Freedom and self-forgetting surrender, we re-cognize our True Self that is always already free, boundless and pure Conscious Presence.

The transformational challenge, as I have been describing in different ways, is to allow all of the permutations of our psychophysical experience to be as they are *without dramatizing them*. Then, through the power of our aspiration, devotion, meditation and inquiry, our contracted self-serving tendencies are scrutinized, penetrated and released. This rhythm of contraction and release keeps on renewing itself, until the impurity has been worked out through deepening self-understanding.

*****

To engage the Divine Test most effectively we have to find the big-heartedness to hold the Great Paradox, which is that this *gradual* process of purification can only fully unfold itself when we simultaneously have the courage to embrace the radical immediacy of our *always already* free True Nature here and now. If we can muster the strength of character and flexibility of mind to embrace this Great Paradox on an ongoing basis, then the Awakening Process will unfold much more quickly and organically.

***** 

We will notice how there is a kind of natural order to what arises for our inspection. In general we will first confront the grosser emotional neurotic tendencies related to the arena of vital life. Our strategies, issues and addictions associated with money, power, work, relationships, food and sex and the associated emotional dramas of shame, guilt, anger, desire and fear will come to the surface of our awareness and assert themselves. That is why a sound basis for true spiritual life has always been the foundational disciplines of a clean and healthy diet, responsible sexuality and, as Gautama Buddha included in his eightfold path, Right Livelihood, Right Speech, Right Action and Right Meditation, to name a few. These disciplines facilitate the Awakening Process by confronting us with all of our neurotic, self-indulgent and dissociative habits, and through the renunciation of those habits of seeking and avoidance the body-mind is balanced and purified.

Once we have faced and transcended the grosser addictive emotional tendencies to a significant degree, then we will tend to confront the deeper constructs of belief, self-image, doubt, arrogance, and all of the narcissistic patterns of self-absorption that compose our characteristic strategy in relationship to life. As this process of self-observation matures we progressively penetrate into the fundamental structure or "holding pattern" of the whirlpool of the ego "I". We begin to observe a particular kind of "face" that we present to others, and a characteristic "role" that our "persona", our "mask", tends to play. We may observe ourselves being characteristically ironic, superficial, aggressive, passive, seductive, etc.

When we have become sensitive to these movements we can then detect the underlying self-image or primary self-sense that shapes our fundamental disposition towards life. For example, one might find that their characteristically tough, or even aggressive stance toward life, is a cover for a constant underlying sense of vulnerability, insecurity or weakness. Or one might find that their social persona of shyness and inferiority is really a cover for a secret sense of superiority or mistrust. Or one might find that the identity of being a nurturing, caring individual who is overly self-sacrificing, is a cover for a deep sense of unworthiness and self-hatred. In general we will discover that our characteristic external strategies are compensations for an inward strategy that might be very different, and perhaps even the opposite, of the face that we present to the world.

*****

When the Awakening Process penetrates to this core level there is often tremendous resistance and friction generated, as we uncover and confront layers of emotional pain that defined the development of our egoic strategy as we grew up. We might even find that there is an entire underworld of phenomena rising up that can be deeply disconcerting and even terrifying, not only because of the intensity of what we are feeling, but also because we do not understand why it is happening and where it is coming from.

If you experience something like what I am describing here then do not be alarmed. As "bad" as it might seem and feel, something very positive and important is happening. The Awakening Process is now penetrating into what is often called "the Shadow" in modern psychology. The Shadow is, by definition, a dimension of our psyche that we cannot see, because it resides outside of the light of our conscious awareness, and that insidiously influences and dictates much of our reactive behaviour from "behind the scenes". Much of what we might term as "neurosis" or "neurotic behaviour" has its invisible roots in the Shadow.

This Shadow aspect of the ego "I" is largely made up of repressed pain that was laid down in childhood when we did not yet have a strong enough sense of individual autonomy to deal with unbearable feelings of loss, abandonment, anger, betrayal, and so on. The Shadow may be particularly evident in more extreme forms in individuals who have suffered sexual and emotional abuse as children. However, while some of us have had a very hard time and some of us an easier time, we all repressed and denied experiences of pain and trauma as we grew up to different degrees. What I am referring to as the Shadow is made up of all that we have judged to be the most dark and undesirable aspects of ourselves, all the unbearable pain and betrayal that we unconsciously denied, repressed and dissociated from, especially as young children, so that we could continue our journey of individuation.

In modern psychiatric terms, the exposure and healing of the Shadow is pursued via the psychotherapeutic process of gaining analytical and emotional knowledge of past trauma. The primary approach of psychotherapy seeks to reclaim knowledge and power for the ego "I" via regressive memory, so that the so-called "causes" of the Shadow neurosis can be identified in the circumstances of infantile and early life, and then relived and potentially released. While it is true that certain levels of trauma and reactive psychophysical pain may be confronted, acknowledged, and then released by such a methodology, the psychotherapeutic approach, in whatever form it takes, can only result in a foundational level of balance and equanimity, not an ultimate cure or healing.

The ultimate healing of our Shadow neurosis involves Awakening from the presumption of being a "wounded self" and its associated presumption of separateness and deficiency. Therefore, the fundamental difference between a psychotherapeutic approach and an authentically spiritual approach toward wholeness and integration, is that in a psychotherapeutic approach *past* circumstances and conditions are seen as the "cause" of our suffering, while in a spiritual approach it is the whirlpool of the self-contraction itself, manifesting in this moment *now* which is recognized to be the ultimate "cause".

While the momentum of past conditioning and reactive patterning is obviously something that we psychologically experience subjectively, once we have Awakened to our True Nature to a significant degree we then have access to a depth dimension of who we are that transcends our psychological self. Then, if we are serious about actualizing that

Awakening, we can no longer insist that past circumstances and conditions were, and still are, the "cause" of our misery. For now we realize that the whirlpool of the ego "I" is not, and never has been, a victim of destiny, and that it is, and always has been, a result of our refusal to love and to abide in our always already Free True Nature. In other words, it is and always has been our *own activity*. This does not necessarily mean that a psychotherapeutic approach and an authentic spiritual approach need to be mutually exclusive in the Awakening Process, because some form of psychotherapy may indeed be essential, especially in the case of individuals who have suffered deep trauma related to various forms of abuse. It simply means that if psychotherapy is necessarily engaged, then when the individual is able to fundamentally demonstrate that psychic integration has been achieved, they can then potentially align, or re-align, themselves with the Source of the Ultimate Cure. Then the newly integrated self acknowledges the *always already* Free Condition in which its individual "healing process" has unfolded.

*****

When the Shadow starts to be illuminated by the searchlight of the Awakening Process, it can erupt like a sudden storm. And when the storm starts coming in what is most essential is to allow the space for these painful emotions to unravel, and to hold fast to our faith and trust in the Process. Then we allow the raw energy of the repressed emotion to transmute like water boiling off into steam. The more conscious we become in our capacity to bear and disentangle ourselves from the intensity of our habitual emotional reactiveness, the more the energy of the emotion will have space to self-liberate and the more that reclaimed energy can then become fuel for further growth and transformation.

Take anger for example, one of the most challenging and "unspiritual" of emotions. There may be all kinds of reasons why anger arises as a repeating pattern. Because there is a common idea in "spiritual" culture that all expressions of anger must be inherently ego-based, we usually repress it, or feel that its presence must mean something negative about us. But it may be very healthy that it is coming up. There is great energy behind anger. If that energy is liberated into its pure, authentic essence what does it become? If we practice bearing witness to our anger without suppressing it, we will find that it often transmutes into a conscious force that is cleanly penetrating, that can cut incisively through confusion into clarity. The authentic energy behind anger is often a fierceness that can be a purifying force of Heat and Light. Of course if we abuse the energy of anger and let ourselves go with it in the wrong way, it turns into aggression and violence, but if we can harness the energy with clear consciousness, then anger can have immense heart in it.

People who have a strong self-image of being a "nice" or "spiritual" person habitually deny and suppress their anger, and as a result often have weak boundaries and collapse under pressure in circumstances that require them to take a strong stand. They might find it very difficult to say a firm and dignified "No!" when it is appropriate and required. Anger can provide the energetic will to change what needs to be changed in a situation; indeed we may need our anger to move forward, to address injustice and to protect the sacredness of life. In the face of injustice, whether individual or collective, anger rouses us to take action – its heat can catalyze the fire of spiritual activism. On the other hand, an ego-based expression of anger is aggressive and seeks to dominate, and to shame and blame the other. So the energy of anger itself can either be completely destructive or a Sacred Fire which manifests spontaneously, as an unfettered expression of intense compassion.

Through valuing the raw energy of our emotions in this way, we can work with them and seek out their liberating essence and free awakened expression. For example, reclaiming the shadow of our childish temper may over time deepen our capacity for clear communication, facing our co-dependent neediness may deepen our capacity for true love and intimacy, and confronting the often wild and confusing terrain of our sexual urges may gradually enable us to discover a truly fulfilling and liberated sexual expression. But all of this is only possible if we are absolutely determined to free ourselves from guilt and shame. Guilt and shame are the demons that keep the shadow caged and so divide us against ourselves. The greater the guilt then the more we usually try to emancipate ourselves by trying to live up to idealized notions of flawless behaviour, and the more we tend to lock ourselves up in either-or, black-white moral thinking.

When we authentically free ourselves from the weight of shame and guilt we release tremendous energy. That energy will then become available to us as a greater capacity to conduct and transmit vitality, discriminating wisdom and emotional intelligence. To transmute these emotions successfully requires patience and perseverance. Besides the essential practices of True Meditation and the ongoing inquiry that is an expression of the Power That Knows The Way, I also suggest physical exercise and bodywork, especially if you are going through an emotionally turbulent period. Emotions that have been habitually repressed over a long period of time get frozen in the nervous system and musculature of the body in the form of constrictions and blockages, so releasing them in that way can also be immensely beneficial.

As we gradually free our emotional nature from chronic patterns of shame, guilt, resentment, rage and jealousy, we discover an increased capacity for clarity, compassion, love and intimacy. We see and feel that in essence we never had a special "personal" problem, and that we never were a fundamentally flawed or wounded self. As we are gradually released from the accumulated pain of our historical story, we are deeply washed and healed by the replenishing balm of Love-Bliss that wells forth as our True Nature. Freshly available to the newness of the moment, we rediscover ourselves unfolding in a joyous dance of integration and release.

*****

When the subject of transcending our emotional experience comes up many people often ask, "What about the emotions of love, joy and peace?" Love, joy and peace are not emotions in the way that I am using the word here. They are feeling qualities that arise, not from the self-contraction of ego, but from the natural radiance of our True Self. Love, joy and peace are qualities of Radiant Being.

It can be helpful when we are endeavoring to distinguish between what is authentic and what is egoic in our experience to make a distinction between emotion and feeling. However, in saying this I am not suggesting that all emotional experience is ego-based, but rather that our emotional experience tends to be deeply habitual, reactive and conditioned. Emotions are subject to the dualistic law of opposites, i.e. there is no pleasure without pain, no excitement without boredom, we go up and then we come down, etc. Many people equate joy with pleasure, but if you closely examine your own experience you will see that pleasure is always derived from the possession and enjoyment of an outside object, whereas joy flows and bubbles up spontaneously from within. What is often called "romantic" love may be pleasurable and exciting for a while, but usually turns into some form of addictive clinging, while true spiritual Love radiates from the Fire of the Heart and has no attachment in it.

The self-contraction of ego denies, and is devoid of, True Love. Yet all human beings long for True Love, and so the ego "I" looks for the love and happiness that it feels is missing "on the inside" in the field of relationships "on the outside". Because it is a spiritual law that one cannot receive what one cannot give, partnerships founded primarily on the mutual attraction of two desiring egos inevitably end in emotional strife and torment, or tend to calcify into the deadening grip of compromise and familiarity, in which the spark of "True Love" is stifled and numbed by the monotony of comfort and convenience.

What is conventionally considered to be love arises from liking and disliking, but True Love transcends this polarity. That is why it is possible to authentically love someone without necessarily liking them. If we are unhappy, then it is because we are attached to what we like and dislike in another or in the world, and as a result we cannot feel the much finer intuitive Feeling of Being that we already are within. When we are no longer attached to our own pain, and the pain of the world, we will find that we don't need the world's pleasure either. We then progressively uncover the natural joy and subtle feeling-intelligence of our innate Being-Consciousness that is ever-present and is the radiant expression of God as Love. As we surrender to the Awakening Process we become more and more capable of being a receiver and a transmitter of this Love, and of seeing everyone and everything as essentially non-separate from our True Self.

The ability to feel in the way I am describing is something much finer and deeper than experiencing changing states of feeling intensity that come and go according to the push and pull of fear and desire. This feeling-intelligence is something that is an innate quality of Consciousness. It is our capacity for sensitivity, for empathy, care and compassion. We might feel sad, as a result of a loss for example, and even shed tears, but this doesn't mean that we are being emotional, that we have identified with, and are being overwhelmed by, the emotion of grief. When we become emotional and disturbed as a consequence, there is usually some subtle or gross degree of self-indulgence occurring. In this way what we may initially experience as an authentic presence of feeling can, if we attach to it, morph and magnify into a wave of emotion, in which we get carried away. When we "get emotional" we become psychically possessed by the emotion that then seems to take on a life of its own.

In general I think it is safe to say that the more we Awaken and Evolve the more we develop our capacity for authentic feeling-intelligence, and thus we gradually free ourselves from habitual emotionality. The deep equanimity that is one of the hallmarks of Spiritual Realization is often interpreted as a state of aloof detachment. However, if that equanimity is founded upon genuine surrender, and not upon a subtle posture of dissociation or spiritual superiority, then that equanimity will incorporate a greater capacity to feel, and a greater ability to respond spontaneously with sensitivity, care and creativity to life, as opposed to the conditioned tendency to withdraw or react emotionally to it.

# Chapter 28

# The Perfection of
# the Process

WE MAY have all kinds of insights and experiences in meditation
and in our life as the Awakening Process progresses. We may experience blazing intuitions, subtle visions, energetic openings and psychic,
extrasensory phenomena of all kinds. On occasion the body may shake,
may feel heat or cold, or may be bathed in radiant bliss. Our senses
may become vibrantly heightened, and at other times our sense of
being in a body may temporarily dissolve completely. But regardless
of what experiences may arise, it is of utmost importance that we do
not allow ourselves to become fascinated and distracted with trying to
extract significance from our experiences.

If we are truly letting everything be as it is, both in our True
Meditation practice and in the unfolding trajectory of our lives, then
whatever insight comes without effort is the significance of any experience, or else perhaps there is no particular significance at all. If we
apparently miss what needs to be learned in one experience, it will
reveal itself again organically in another. This Process continues until

the lesson we need has been learned. When our aspiration for spiritual freedom is profound and continuous we will find that this Awakening Process will bring whatever we have to learn into our conscious awareness. And when we are ready to learn something we will usually find that we see it everywhere.

Practiced with sincere heartfelt aspiration, the regular practice of True Meditation activates an organic self-transcending process of purification and growth. It is like spring rain falling on the fertile ground where an acorn is lying. The acorn sprouts and begins to root itself in the soil and then commences its remarkable journey of reaching out into the sky and becoming a tree. In this metaphor, the roots reaching down into the soil represent our practice of becoming more and more deeply grounded in the prior Freedom and Happiness of our ever-present Being. The upward growth of the tree represents the unfolding emergence of our individuated humanity reaching into its unique expression of the innate unity, love and intelligence of Consciousness in time and space.

In this organic process of growth each deepening insight serves as a releasing mechanism, like a key that unlocks another layer of our ignorance and unconsciousness. We only need to have faith, trust and surrender in this Process. We will know intuitively if we are growing, but we do not need to know what is happening. When we have understood deeply that the limited mechanism of the mind can never figure out or grasp this Process, then we will let go of looking for any particular significance from our experiences. Because we are living in a fundamental disposition of trust, we will no longer need any proof or any kind of validation that we are "getting somewhere". And when we let go of the need to measure our progress in any way whatsoever we will be delighted to discover that the Awakening Process speeds up considerably.

We will progressively understand that the depth and purity of the Awakening Process is simply determined by what we are willing to learn in any moment. We begin to recognize that we see what we *desire to see* and, whether that desire is conscious or unconscious, we tend to justify our prejudices, presumptions and projections. So if we truly want to be Free we will let go of trying to see anything in particular. Our challenge is to accept everything as it is without qualification, and then see what comes.

*****

It is a spiritual law that the authenticity of our Awakening has to be Realized – made real – by living it, thus we will be confronted with the Divine Tests, and also all of the circumstances and teachers needed to aid us in the Awakening Process will be provided. In the earlier stages of the Process our awareness of this essential cohesive intelligence in the unfolding of our life is rarely apparent, except in flashes, because we are still so identified with our conflicting emotions and our desires and fears. But as we mature in faith, trust and surrender, the thread of an unmistakable purpose, which infuses our individual life with significance, is more and more deeply recognized and felt.

Understanding that every liberating insight has to be tested and grounded in the circumstances and events of our ongoing life, ennobles us with a certain detachment from events. We tend to identify less with the drama or pressure of what may be happening in our life at any given time. Thus, according to the depth of our Awakening, we suffer less and, as we look back, we glimpse the incredible precision and Perfection of the Process.

Through ever-deepening understanding of this Perfection we progressively relinquish the illusion of personal control. As we let go of the illusion of personal control by consistently offering this precious human life to the Fire of the Heart, we ensure that we will go as far as possible in the Awakening Process in this incarnation. There is literally nothing more that any of us can do than that. Then Consciousness, Spirit, God – whatever name most resonates with us for the ultimate Mystery that we *are* – takes care of the rest and our trust in the Perfection of the Process only deepens.

# Part VI

# DEEPER DIVES

# Chapter 29

# The Path and the Goal
# Are One

THE DIVINE Test that we face in each and every moment in relation to the content of our experience, is our reckoning with the law of self-sacrifice. When we surrender to this law we are liberated, we are brightened, and we are ennobled, because we are living the Truth of Freedom here and now, at the highest level of responsibility that we are capable of. Then we can embrace the Great Paradox that the Path and the Goal are One – Happiness, Fullness and Freedom is our True Nature here and now, *and* we are an evolutionary Work-In-Progress.

It is worth reflecting a little further upon this matter of the Path and the Goal being One, because it is not the common orientation in either traditional spirituality or progressive "alternative" spirituality in the West. Within many spiritual traditions, and their postmodern offshoots, one will often find the "sudden school" teachers and teachings, that emphasize the Goal, and the "gradual school" teachers and teachings, that emphasize the Path.

The sudden school teachers and teachings tend to point exclusively to the Absolute Truth that we are already Free, that the whirlpool of the ego "I" is an illusion, and that the Goal of Awakening is always already the case. The essence of their invitation can be summarized in the phrases "Be Here Now" or "Realize and Surrender". Teachers and teachings emphasizing the "sudden" side of the street are generally very popular with Westerners who want to imbibe the most profound Enlightenment teachings that come to us from the East, while bypassing any rigorous purifying discipline, and the challenging, and sometimes terrifying, ordeals of burning in the Fire of the Heart and submitting to the Divine Tests.

There is a whole spectrum of depth, authenticity and purity in "sudden school" teachers and teachings, which is beyond the scope of this book to explore, however the common orientation in all of them is the directing of attention beyond egoic self-consciousness to the Transcendent Self or Consciousness beyond all conditions. Because they tend to value Transcendence over Transformation, Being over Becoming, the passive, static pole of Consciousness over the dynamic, active pole, many "sudden school" teachers make little or no demand on their students, other than to relinquish all forms of seeking, and so they tend to not recommend any purifying disciplines. This often results in a situation in which students may have access to consistent Awakenings in the presence of the teacher, but who then tend to fall back into the habitual patterns of self-contraction when they go back to their everyday lives. Indeed, some of these teachers and teachings even go as far as to assert that authentic Awakening has no relationship whatsoever to the body-mind, and they therefore contend that Awakening does not necessarily have any transformative impact on the self-expression of the individual, or any significant implications for how a human life is lived in the world. Also, because of the valuing of Transcendence over Transformation, such teachers often take a "no position" position of "not wanting to create anything" in relationship with their students, and so they explicitly avoid any association with the formal system-ization of practices and the development of any structure to support the emergence of a spiritual culture. This orientation tends to suit the typical hyper-individualized Western seeker, who wants to "get enlightened" while maintaining his or her own autonomy, and who is often suspicious of hierarchy and of any kind of perceived "group mind" that might threaten his or her sense of independence.

Then, there are the "gradual school" teachers and teachings that emphasize and lay out a Path, through which we may gradually trans-form ourselves through a dedicated daily regimen of meditation, prayer, contemplation and study, conscious exercise and pure diet etc. Their invitation can be summarized in the phrases "Just do the Practice" or "Purify Thyself". The teachers and teachings on the "gradual" side of the street tend to occur within existing spiritual traditions, and also tend to emphasize the teaching over, or as much as, the teacher. In general the "gradual schools" are popular with more con-ventionally minded, conformist individuals who are attracted to the time-honoured depth of a traditional wisdom stream, and willingly embrace disciplines, rituals and practices as "skillful means" on the way to the Goal of spiritual liberation.

The limitation of the "sudden school" approach, driven as it is by the ideal of liberation from the conditioning of the body-mind, is that the concerns of the individual psyche become insignificant, and its structures are viewed as something to be transcended as quickly as possible. Despite the fact that all self-transcending methods will cause a degree of self-transformation, in general the "sudden" orientation does not entail a concerted effort to illuminate and purify the deeply embedded motivational patterning of the ego. Hence, much of what we explored in the chapter "Light on Shadow" is bypassed and psychic integration is usually not accomplished. Without a commitment to consistent purification and practice, the sudden school can easily become a "talking school"(as Spiritual Master Adi Da called it), in which Awakening is taught and envisioned in a way that is largely conceptual and disembodied. When there is this inherent bias that values Transcendence over Transformation to a gross or subtle degree, then even if the Awakening that is being transmitted is authentic, its implications usually do not "trickle down" to infuse, and potentially reconfigure, all the dimensions of the human being. As a result of this orientation an individual might have some degree of authentic knowledge of, and penetration into, Transcendent Being, but may still be very much bound in their self-expression by the biological, psychological and cultural conditioning of the body-mind.

On the other hand, the primary limitation with the "gradual" approach is that in its emphasis on practice and development along a linear line of time, it inevitably tends to lose touch with the radical immediacy of Freedom here and now, and therefore tends to perpetuate the act of seeking.

*****

The orientation of the Awakening Process that I am endeavoring to share with you in this book is an approach that embraces the paradox of the Path and the Goal and transcends its polarity. Through consistent aspiration, trust, faith and surrender we could metaphorically say that we reach *upwards* in a gesture of Ascent, opening ourselves to the radical immediacy of Transcendent Consciousness here and now. And through our commitment to Transformation, to the *Realization* of our Awakening, we also reach *downwards* in a gesture of Descent, of deeply respecting, honouring and making room for the slower-moving processes of purification, through which so many of the intermediate dimensions of the psychophysical being are organically realigned and transfigured.

In our attunement to the ever-present *Goal* here and now, we open ourselves up to the Mystery in surrendered receptivity. In our conscious engagement with the *Path* we work hard to purify ourselves. Without purifying effort there will be no foundation to receive the gift of Grace, which is the spontaneous inflow of understanding and inspiration. And without our receptivity to Grace, our self-effort is destined to remain barren.

*****

This commitment to ever-deepening Realization, in the context of embracing the Path and the Goal as One, is a continuous matter of surrender that *transcends and includes* all of the conditions of the body-mind, and the world in which it appears. Only if we endeavor to integrate Path *and* Goal, Heaven *and* Earth, Ascent *and* Descent, Transcendence *and* Transformation, and Being *and* Becoming, can the Awakening Process unfold in its full fruition.

In our practical moment to moment experience, this means allowing for the fact that we live in a gross form associated with a gross realm, in which we often experience primitive states of consciousness, as well as higher and more subtle states of consciousness, and that these conditions tend to be limiting. Through accepting that we do not have the option to dissociate from the grosser aspects of our nature, we can see that the (characteristically Eastern) Path of Ascent that seeks the Goal in an otherworldly "Heaven" or "Nirvana", is a strategy of the spiritualized ego "I" that seeks to escape from or exclude the relative reality of Life and Earth. Similarly, we can see that the (characteristically Western) Path of Descent, that envisions the fulfillment of the Goal in terms of "good works" and the creation of some kind of utopian evolutionary potential on Earth, often leads to idealistic notions of the perfection of our humanity, and "saving the world", that inevitably end in frustration and disappointment.

The orientation of Descent tends to be prevalent in the West for two reasons. The first reason is the traditional association between historical Christianity and the idea (beginning with the myths, associated with Jesus of Nazareth) of the Spiritualization of human physical existence and the eventual coming of the Kingdom of Heaven to Earth. Even if, as Westerners, we do not consider ourselves to be Christians, and we may regard the resurrection of Jesus Christ as a myth, our spiritual sensibility still usually tends to view the implications of Spiritual Awakening in earthly terms. The second reason has its seed in the Renaissance and European Enlightenment of the sixteenth and seventeenth centuries, which gave birth to the modernist "faith" in human progress, driven by the technological innovations of science. This cultural zeitgeist was further bolstered in the nineteenth and twentieth centuries by the cosmological and biological evolutionary narratives that emerged from science, that strongly suggested that Creation was a directional Process unfolding along a line of time. These two Western orientations towards the Spiritualization and Perfection of Man, and the progressive perfection of human society, are often blended in more progressive and contemporary spiritual movements, driven by an "evolutionary idealism" which seeks to support the common hopefulness relative to physical and social existence. But because the actual results of such "Paths of Descent" apply, in general, only to the ordinary mental, emotional, physical, and social sphere, they sometimes amount to little more than an overstated form of utopian idealism.

In authentic Awakening there is of course a powerful call to transform the world into an expression of the Great Perfection we have discovered to be its Source. But if our Awakening is truly profound, there will also be the recognition that that Great Perfection is *only* experienced in the *Awakening to That Transcendent Source*, not in relationship to the particularities of the display of manifest existence that arise as a *modification* of that Source. The attainment of some kind of static Perfection is not achievable in a Creation that is defined by dynamic polarities, and that is in constant flux in every dimension. Thus, while we may experience an authentic passion to "bring Heaven to Earth" and play our part in evolving this world, we also understand that this world is not, and never will be, a humanly-conceived utopia, and is not designed or destined to be a Heaven. When we rest as Consciousness Itself, the entire display of manifest existence is no longer conceived as a conflicted drama between good and evil. And in place of being ensnared in this conflicted drama of opposites, a world-transcending wideness and equanimity dawns like a wide-open sky, that transcends and includes all of the "weather" of phenomena that appears in it. This equanimity, if it is truly Free, is not a detached, aloof disposition of dissociation and aversion to the Life Process. Rather it is an equanimity that radiates like a Great Sun. This wide sunlit equanimity is inherently free of the "gravitational pull" or "centrifugal force" of phenomenal self-awareness. And so, from that vantage point, this world of changes is perceived to be more like a "school" than a conflicted Hell realm, or a potential utopia or Heaven. It is recognized as a school that is purposed toward ego-transcendence, for those who are willing to learn, and in that school the entire spectrum of possibilities, from the most horrific to the most sublime, play out via endless causes and effects.

The Western orientation of Descent tends to imagine that God, Spirit, the Divine Reality, has withdrawn from the world as a result of human "sin". However, the Truth is that God has never withdrawn for God is the Source and Sustainer of the world. God, Spirit, the Divine Reality, is *already here* as the fundamental Condition of the world, for the created world is nothing other than a patterning and densification of God's Light. This is why if God, Spirit, the Divine Reality, is not presently *lived*, there can be no Second Coming, no Revelation, no Salvation, no Enlightenment, no Nirvana. However, if humankind would begin to live authentically in, and as, the Truth of Prior Unity, then we could see a vast and immediate Transformation of the world.

*****

Recognizing and understanding that our individual body-mind and the appearance of the world are the manifest expression of God or Consciousness does *not mean* that the individual or world can or should *become* a "perfect reflection" of the Divine Reality. Nor does it mean that conditional existence *and* the unconditioned Transcendent Reality are both *equally* necessary. That conviction or belief would imply that the unconditioned Transcendent Reality, and the conditional appearance of the individual and world are necessarily *always* coincident, and *inherently* identical. If that were the case then the conditional appearances of the individual and the world, would have to be perpetuated *ad infinitum* for the full fruition of the Conscious Freedom, Happiness, and Love of the Awakening Process to Reveal Itself. A simple metaphor that may help in understanding this, is that of a mirror. The mirror – the unconditioned Transcendent Consciousness – is one, or coincident, with the conditional phenomena of body, mind and world that appears within it. The appearance of phenomena cannot be separated out from the mirror, and so in this sense the mirror and the phenomena reflected within it are identical, and so they are Non-Dual, meaning not one and not two. But when the phenomena of body, mind and world changes or disappears, the mirror itself is unchanged and unaffected. Thus, the unconditioned and the conditioned, the mirror and the reflected phenomena, are not *inherently* identical, and they are not *always* coincident.

If Awakening to our True Identity as Consciousness Itself is truly profound, we will intuitively see and know that the appearance of our individual body-mind and the world is a *projection* of Consciousness Itself, and thus, as an evolving individual organ of that Consciousness, we will increasingly feel the pain of the whole, and the joy of the whole, as our own pain and our own joy. This is why, we will be spontaneously moved to bring the Goodness, Truth and Beauty that we have recognized into manifestation through our creative response to life. That movement in Consciousness is what the Power That Knows The Way *Is*. We could say it is what the Power That Knows The Way *wants*. But a liberated response to the pain of this world can only spring forth when we are essentially *undivided*, when we are resting in the intuitive knowledge of Prior Unity, that sees the whole display of Creation as already perfect *as it is* in its play of opposites, in its constant dynamic of the birth and death of countless beings. Then, we are both essentially already *free from* the world and, paradoxically, we are available to participate *fully in* the world, without any binding attachment to a particular outcome or result in time and space.

In the most profound depths of the Non-Dual Revelation, the appearance of the conditional individual body-mind and the world, are seen and felt to be transparent, and inherently non-binding, limitations that are interpenetrated by the inherent Radiance of Consciousness and Love-Bliss Itself. And in that heartfelt recognition, those apparently limiting conditions no longer make any fundamental "difference".

This integral, "full spectrum" understanding transcends both the (characteristically Western) error of embracing the individual body-mind and world with a view to the fulfillment of a utopian ideal of "Spiritualized Perfection" or "Heaven on Earth", and the (characteristically Eastern) error of dissociation from, or exclusion of, the individual body-mind and world, via the paths of Ascent or the strategic inversion of attention.

By wholeheartedly endeavoring to unite the Path and the Goal and the Ascending and Descending streams of wisdom in this integral embrace, we will develop the capacity to progressively shift our being, on all levels, into the Reality of the Heart. And in so doing, our individual body-mind will be progressively forged into a Heart-Free messenger of the Divine, that spontaneously expresses our deepest understanding and calling.

*****

We will know that the ascending stream of the Divine is authentically alive within us when we begin to experience a widening, and a deepening into, the Witnessing Consciousness. In that relaxed equanimity, our natural inclination is to rest in resonant attunement with What Is, without struggle and without strategy.

We will know that the descending stream of the Divine is authentically alive within us when we begin to experience an emanation of Love flowing through our psychophysical being, that embraces everything that we are, in all our imperfection, and everything that the world is, in all its imperfection. We will *feel* nourished by this Love, and we will find within ourselves all the humility, patience and courage that is needed to endure the challenges of the Divine Tests and actualize our deepest potential, even in the face of all the resistive remnants of ego growling in our psyche. And, to the degree that we surrender, we will also feel that Love radiating out to embrace all beings and the multifaceted display of manifest Creation.

*****

Embracing the Path *and* the Goal, Transcendence *and* Transformation, Heaven *and* Earth, Ascent *and* Descent, keeps us wide open and yielded to *Di-vine* Communion. We invoke, "pull down" and "plug into" Transcendent Freedom as our intuited True Nature, while simultaneously living in humble relationship to our conscious participation in the purgatory fires of purification, and to our own evolution as a perpetually unfolding Work-In-Progress.

So will you love the Divine Source, Condition and Totality in which you are arising, even now at this very moment? Will you fall on your knees in awe, wonder and submission before the call of the Great Awakening Process? Or will you turn away from THAT and continue to be held captive by the contracted whirlpool of the ego "I"?

If you have seen beyond the veil of separate personhood, if you have discovered the ever-present Transcendental I AM Presence as your True Self, then will you take the next step into the Fire of the Heart, and willingly allow yourself to Feel the Heat? Will you allow yourself to be burned clean by Its Flames? Will you yield yourself to the Divine Tests, so that you can lend your Heart-Light to the Great Process?

What will you do? Surrender or withdraw? That is the Divine Test that confronts you in every moment. Why not submit yourself to what is *obviously* True, Good and Beautiful, with as much energy and passion as you can summon? And then, see what you *Realize.*

# Chapter 30

# Meditation Is Not What You Think

As we go deeper into True Meditation and the Awakening Process we find that we are increasingly less and less bothered by the modifications of mind. Once we have fundamentally ceased to take the reportage of our mind so seriously, we can then gain profound and liberating insight into the mechanism of thinking itself. So I now want to invite you to take a deeper dive with me into this matter of thinking from the vantage point of the understanding that we have been immersed in thus far...

Who is it that is thinking, thinking, thinking? What is thought and what is mind really? Is it not true that the only thought that we are actually aware of is the thought that is appearing right now? Despite the fact that so many of us complain and feel victimized by our "busy minds", the truth is that we can only have one thought at a time. If we can have only one thought at a time, what exactly is "mind" and where is it located?

Apply yourself consistently to the practice of True Meditation accompanied by Self-Inquiry into the question "Who am I?", and it will soon become self-evident, that what we refer to as "my" mind obviously has no substantial existence at all, and yet the vast majority of human beings never slow down enough to discover this fact. Much of what we habitually refer to as "my mind" is simply patterns of remembered perceptions in the brain. Where is the Truth and the Reality in that?

If our True Nature as Consciousness Itself is the source of all true intelligence and sensitivity, then why do we think, think and think endlessly? Even if we live a very ascetic or balanced lifestyle and we could reasonably say that we have transcended most, if not all, of our physical and emotional addictions to the repetition and exploitation of experience, are we not still addicted to endless thinking? What is it that motivates and drives this almost interminable stream of thought that we are involved in?

As I have already discussed from numerous angles, Consciousness is our irreducible Identity that is prior to the appearance of mind. Mind is a modification of Consciousness, like waves are a modification of the ocean. But when we "fall" from inherence in our True Self as Consciousness into exclusive identification with mind, we literally believe that *we are what we think*. The ocean believes that it is the wave. And when we believe that we are what we think we become bound to an insidious form of artificial intelligence.

By artificial intelligence I mean that instead of True Intelligence, which is a tacit, intrinsically wordless, direct, spontaneous, living contact with life and phenomena as they arise, we instead perceive Reality through the symbolic representations of a language program that is conditioned by the past. It might appear strange to call the mind a "language program" because we presume that we only use language when we are speaking, but when we are not speaking and thought is occurring we are effectively talking to ourselves. Thought is largely internalized language, even when it is in the form of imagery. Thus, when we perceive *what is* through the prism of mind, our interpretation of Reality is a re-presentation of the past in the form of thought or internalized language, and this constant re-presentation of the past programs our brain and patterns our interactions with existence.

There is a famous line from a poem by Gertrude Stein that says, "A rose is a rose is a rose". The whole point being that every word is a symbol that points to, but can never capture or communicate, what the essence of a thing actually is in and of itself. Even though language is purely symbolic, when we identify with mind as self we literally invent a symbolic destiny for ourselves through the repetition of particular stories, self-images, beliefs and obsessions. We lose touch with the vibrant, fresh, ungraspable incandescence of Reality *as it is*, and instead live in a mediocre, dumbed down, perceptual "fog" of familiarity.

Through the constant re-presentation of mental symbols, we concretize our self-identity and project that identity and its imagined destiny into an idea of time and space beyond the present moment. Hence, we could say that we all live in a "virtual reality" of mind, effectively self-identified with the artificial intelligence of a robot.  This mind machine, that replicates language forms and constantly re-presents the past, creates the illusion of a substantial, continuous "I" that we associate with the mortal body-mind complex of our embodied individuality.  Spiritual Master Adi Da describes this phenomenon with incisive precision:

> *Mind is an interior projection of a language-program that, in its imaginative elaboration of itself, conceives of purposes and ideas (in the realm of illusion) for which there are no corresponding physical data. Human beings are all living in a "virtual world" of mind. Human beings are, characteristically, egoically "self"-identified with a "robot", an artificial intelligence.*

Looked at developmentally, we can see that our learning how to speak was coincident with the development of our verbal mind. This development occurred so that we could communicate in the expanding field of our relations as we grew up. But then, when there was nobody there to talk to, we became enamored with this newfound capacity and we kept talking to ourselves. We somehow got addicted to our own self-reflection in and through the verbal mind, through symbolic language, which of course became more and more complex as we grew up.

Of course there are many other dimensions to the activity of mind that are essential and valuable to our full expression and functioning as human beings. There is the functional capacity of mind that enables us to comprehend, plan and deduct practically and rationally. There is the differentiating capacity of mind that enables us to discriminate and discern. And there is what we could call the intuitive capacity of mind, that arises on the wings of a pure creative impulse and enables us to communicate, to paint, to make music, to dance and to write etc. All of these forms of mental activity are signs of a healthy adaption to life, in which the mind is employed as a willing servant or tool. But if we apply ourselves to a continuous process of True Meditation and self-observation, we will probably discover that most of our habitual mental activity does not take any of these forms, rather it takes the form of us having an almost continuous conversation with ourselves.

Now does this strike you as somewhat crazy? Think about it. It should be apparent, if you have read this far, that there is in fact nobody in there! Through immersing ourselves in True Meditation and opening up to Wide Open Wonder we have discovered that there is no inward, subjective "I" or thinker distinct from thought itself that can be located. So this must mean that our habitual mode of more or less continuous self-referential thinking is an addiction to the illusion of relatedness with someone who does not actually exist!

When we dream at night we multiply ourselves into all kinds of beings and scenes, but on waking we realize that there was really no one there. When we go into deep sleep there is literally no one there and what a profound relief and relaxation that is. Then we wake up in the morning, and if we spent a long time with "nobody there" in deep sleep, we say, "Ah "I" slept so well!" And then the artificial intelligence program immediately kicks into gear, with its interiorized speech mind to continue the fascinating adventure, or bad soap opera, of "me" and "my" life.

Our addiction to our self-referencing interiorized speech mind prevents most of us from ever experiencing True Aloneness, by which I mean True All-One-Ness. The mechanism of self-referential mind keeps us involved in a social situation constantly. Think about what you mean when you say something like, "I thought to myself..." Who are you talking to? Who are you thinking to?

Here is a riddle to contemplate: if you are the one who is going to receive the thought, then why did you have to think it in the first place?

This unquestioned habit of turning in upon ourselves by thinking, thinking, thinking is the whirlpool in the ocean that we presume to be our "natural state", and so it whirls on automatic pilot. But if we closely examine our experience we will see, even if only momentarily, that this apparently natural and normal state of affairs is based on a false presumption.

As we have already explored, our True Nature is Consciousness Itself, the ever-present I AM that transcends and includes all phenomena and all opposites. Resting as THAT we dis-cover the One without a second, the Non-Dual Reality that transcends and includes the phenomenal world of duality and multiplicity. When we rest in and as Consciousness Itself, whether it is a glimpse or a prolonged abidance, there is *no other* to speak of. All apparent others and objects are seen to arise in and as permutations of One Consciousness, like the waves on the ocean. But as soon as we "fall" into identification with the self-referential activity of mind, as soon as we forget our Prior Unity as the ocean and turn inwardly upon ourselves into the whirlpool, we morph and contract, and get locked into the world of duality and separateness, which always presumes two or more.

This "fall" into duality does not happen simply because thoughts arise, it happens when we collapse into the whirlpool by *identifying* with them, when we believe in them, for then we give them *power*. But when we stand Free as the I AM Presence, that calm abiding does not stimulate more mental activity. As the Witness we observe the compulsion to engage in the self-referential momentum of our inner dialogue in any moment, and in that observation there is a deepening understanding and potential transcendence of that activity.

One way to understand the moment of understanding is that the self-perpetuating loop or link that holds the illusion of the inner dialogue together is dissolved. Thus, as our meditation and inquiry deepens over time, we progressively free our energy and attention from the cycling loop of narcissistic self-infatuation. Then, while self-referential thought may still arise due to the momentum of conditioning, the "thinker", or the presumed "I" at the center to whom those thoughts habitually refer, is more and more often absent. In this way the centrifugal force of the whirlpool uncoils, and the incessant self-referential mental activity loses its magnetism. We find that we are less and less preoccupied with the endless psychological "mind movies" about "me" and how "I" feel about "my" life. As we free our energy and attention in this way we become more and more comfortable with not needing to know who we are in the "I" of our mind, to authentically and spontaneously *be* who we are in every moment. Released from the narcissistic patterning of the whirlpool, we feel widened, spacious, light and vibrant, and ecstatically merged into unmitigated communion with Reality as it is.

# Chapter 31

# There Is No Other

To FACILITATE this process of freeing ourselves from the whirlpool of narcissism it is useful to ask ourselves periodically, "Why do I always want to exist as if I am in dialogue with someone else, when there is really no one else there? Why do I impose this fabrication on Reality? Why am I so trapped in a closed loop that, on close inspection, reveals itself to be an absurdity?"

Do you remember when we took a brief tour through our psychophysical development from babyhood to adulthood in the second chapter of the book called *Growing Up*? We saw how the primitive, infantile basis of the contraction of the ego "I" was based on the need to be fed, to relieve the trauma of our "fall" into vulnerable embodiment. That pre-conscious feeling of relatedness as we were sucking at our mother's breast, laid down the template for the further elaboration of our self-contraction. So if we extrapolate that template out to mature adulthood, we can see that strong patterns of addiction and dependency around food, sex and relationships are expressions of seeking fulfillment through the essentially infantile craving for union and safety. Feeding creates a pleasurable sensation in the baby's body, a feeling that makes the baby feel comfortable, sustained, and protected, and adults get a similar satisfaction from sex. Sex is a way of "feeding" on energy. It makes us feel good because it is contact with life-energy. However, just as breastfeeding makes the baby feel dependent for life-energy on the source of food that is outside it, so sex makes us feel that we are dependent on having sex to get life-energy.

For more developed adults, the center of gravity tends to be in the adolescent mode of a sense of relatively mature autonomy, that is intent on seeking fulfillment through ever-widening circles of experience and knowledge. And if we extrapolate this template all the way to this subtle consideration of mind, we can see that the constant automatic activity of self-referential thinking is itself a form of addiction to the presumption of an "other", even when there is no other here!

So it may be helpful as you witness your mental chattering, both in meditation practice and throughout your daily life, to simply bring this understanding to bear on what is occurring. Just consider that the reason that you are not getting any peace is because this illusory "other" fascinates you. Your self-referential thinking presumes that there is somebody else there and without that well, who would you be?

Be aware of when you react to suffering, as if someone else is there, by moving into blaming others or circumstances. Then you are acting like a child. Observe when you project your idea of God outside of yourself, and pursue a relationship with Him or Her, or "the Universe", in which you believe that He or She, or "the Universe", is looking out for you *personally*. Then again, you are acting like a child. You are projecting the illusion of relationship onto the Absolute Reality, and so you are still presuming that a Big Daddy or Mommy in the sky parents you. The more you pierce through the artificial intelligence programming in this way, the more it will become clear that the habitual activity of self-referential thinking *is* the activity of self-contraction and *is* the whirlpool turning in upon itself.

If you let this in very deeply, you might find that your thinking significantly slows down or even comes to a halt for a significant astonished interval. You may notice that you stop indulging in the conversation. You may begin to recognize that so much habitual thinking is pure nonsense and completely unnecessary, and you may notice that you become capable of standing in the naked unity of Pure Existence. You also become aware that you are Happy. Instantaneously! Ah could there be a connection?

In the earlier and intermediate stages of the Awakening Process, much of our practice is directed toward the transcendence of our habits of isolation and withholding. As we abide in True Meditation and, through making ourselves available to the Power That Knows The Way, we lean toward the conscious embrace of the truth of our interrelatedness, we transcend certain limits and begin to creatively engage with life and learn to love others in ways that were previously inhibited. But the *relative* truth of our interrelatedness with all others rests upon a deeper *Absolute* Truth, which is the Non-Dual Revelation that ultimately *there is no other*. In that mighty Knowledge-Vision, we directly see that there is no locatable line of separation and no locatable boundary of limitation anywhere, and therefore there is ultimately nothing to relate to. To the degree that we recognize the Absolute Truth that *there is no other*, we are freed from the illusion of relatedness, and therefore freed from the need to be completed and fulfilled by any other person, activity, object, otherworldly Deity, or any experience whatsoever.

When we meditate and investigate very deeply, it becomes clear that the presumption of a subjective inner "I" is not an authentic connection to experience. We also discover that the re-presentation of knowledge based on the past is actually an avoidance of direct experience. We realize that we are only truly connected to our experience when we abide in not knowing or Wide Open Wonder, which is the relinquishment of the mental prison of artificial intelligence that can only re-present the past. And then, paradoxically, we discover that in Reality we are not "connected", because there is no "I" to be connected with anything. Rather there is Divine Communion with All That Is. All forms are seen to be modifications of that Great One. "You" and "I" are not related to that One, we *are* that One. There is Only One of us here. I am You and You are Me. Literally.

# Chapter 32

# Be Here Now

"Be Here Now" is a very popular spiritual slogan these days, originally popularized by the book "Be Here Now" written by Ram Dass, in the midst of the hippy movement and the first wave of the Enlightenment teachings coming from the East to the West in the early seventies. And more recently the huge popularity of Eckhart Tolle's bestselling book "The Power of Now" has catapulted this spiritual notion into the mainstream.

Many spiritual teachers and teachings speak about the importance of being "in the present moment" or "in the Now", as a way to catalyze an Awakening to the ever-present Witness or pure sense of I AM. This direct "pointing" can indeed be a very potent catalyst for Awakening. However, there is sometimes a limitation inherent in such an approach in that the "present moment" often tends to be interpreted as a momentary slice of time occurring between the two vast expanses of the past and future. Hence the "present moment" or "Now" is usually conceptualized as a moment of very short duration moving along a line of time.

As a result of this interpretation spiritual seekers and meditators might engage in an effortful manipulation of their experience to keep

their attention focused on this fleeting slice of time. People who inter-
pret "being in the moment" in this way might conclude, for example,
that speaking about the past or making any concrete future plans is
"unenlightened" behaviour, or that not being able to remember where
one put one's car keys automatically means that one was "not-in-the-
Now" and lost in one's ego. Often seekers who do a lot of mindfulness
techniques or vipassana meditation fall into this trap of self-consciously
practising "living-in-the-present-moment".

However, True Freedom, Happiness and Peace can never be experienced through self-conscious techniques or manipulation of any kind,
because the one who is "trying to be aware" is the self-referencing ego
"I" that is engaged in the futile task of trying to go beyond itself. The
ego "I" is very persistent and insidious and can take all kinds of subtle
"spiritualized" forms. It will attempt to hijack our spiritual trajectory in devious ways so that it can maintain covert control, however
subtly, over the body-mind and subvert the organic unfolding of the
Awakening Process. This is why our one pointed clarity of intention
and courageous surrender to this Process is so essential, because only
then will we progressively develop the capacity to observe, understand
and transcend, the ever more subtle survival strategies of the ego "I",
that always wants to come along for the spiritual ride and attend its
own funeral!

*****

The spiritual injunction to Be Here Now is a very profound teaching
with radical implications if we are willing to take it all the way. It has

far greater implications than directing our attention to stay focused in the present moment. Indeed, it has the potential to completely turn our habitual relationship to time and space upside down and inside out, and in so doing catapult us into an awe-inspiring depth of profundity and revelation.

Our usual experience of life is that we think that we perceive time and space outside our self, and that we are limited creatures that exist for a short time in the vast duration of time, and that occupy a very small part of a vast expanse of space. However, though time and space appear to exist "outside", we actually have no way of knowing that they do exist outside or independent of our Consciousness. In fact no human being, or any sentient being for that matter, has ever experienced a world of time and space outside of its own self-awareness.

If we simply abide as the I AM Presence, and observe the seeming reality of time, we will soon recognize that if we have a thought or image about the past or the imagined future, then that thought or image is always experienced *now*. In the intimacy of our own ever-present Being, which is prior to thought, we only know *now*, we never actually know the past or future. While our experience of now can include memories and imagined futures we never, in fact, leave the present moment. On closer inspection, we will realize that the idea that we ever could leave or "lose touch" with the present moment is absurd. Can we choose to step out of the Now? Where would we go? Where could we go? Is this "present moment" going anywhere in time? Can this "present moment" travel backwards and forwards in time? No! Because the "present moment" is not actually a moment in time.

While all that passes by is constantly changing, the present moment itself always remains without undergoing any change, hence we could describe it as the static doorway through which we may pass from the relative reality of ever-changing present time, to the Absolute Reality of our unchanging Being.

If the present is the only moment in time that truly exists, and that we can experience directly and actually, then what is often called the "present moment" must be ever-present. Even to speak then, of the "present moment" is potentially misleading, because time is actually a continuous flow that does not consist of discrete units called "moments". A moment is just a conceptual fraction of time, a fraction whose duration is arbitrary, depending on what we are referring to when we speak about the "present moment".

To take the inquiry further ask yourself, "What in my experience is ever-present and unchanging? Are the appearances of the body, the mind, the personality and the world ever-present and unchanging?" With a little curiosity and observation it becomes obvious that in the waking state the body, the mind, the personality and the world are changing all the time. Then, when we enter into dream at night, we take on a dream body that appears in a dream world that seems as real as the body and world we experience in the waking state. When the dream state dissolves and we merge into deep sleep, all bodies and worlds disappear. Yet even though we appear to be unconscious in deep sleep we wake up in the morning and feel that "I slept well" or, if we did not experience sufficient deep sleep, we feel that "I didn't sleep well".

Only Consciousness Itself that transcends and includes the three states of waking, dreaming and deep sleep, is ever-present and un-changing. How could it be otherwise? Therefore, while we appear in the waking state to be an individual body-mind arising within the world, the deeper truth is that our individual body-mind and the ap-parently "outside world" are appearing *within us* as Consciousness Itself. We are not present *in* the now; we *are* the Now! The Now is not a pre-existing container in which we, as an individual body-mind and the world, appear. The Now is the Light of Consciousness Itself, that static doorway, in and through which the entire field of experience appears in a seamless, continuous flow. Thus, the more that we root ourselves in the injunction to Be Here Now and abide in and as the I AM Presence, the more that the "present moment" reveals itself to be all pervading and encompassing of *all time*.

Similarly just as the present moment "now" is the central point in the conceptual dimension of time, so the present place "here" is the central point in the conceptual dimension of space. Every point in space that we perceive or can think of exists only with reference to the present place, the point in space at which we now feel ourselves to be.

Because we identify ourselves with a body, we feel that we move about in space, but in fact space moves about within us. Wherever we appear to go, the present space of "here" is always with us. When we seem to move from one place to another, the next place becomes "here". Thus, just as the present moment "now" is the static and unchanging timeless moment through which all the moments of time pass, so the present place, "here", is the static and unchanging placeless place through which we may pass from the relative reality of being a body that moves about in space, to the Absolute Reality of our unmoving Being.

If we inquire into the truth that is revealed in the simple injunction to Be Here Now in our own direct experience, we will discover that the idea that the "present moment" is a point in time is an illusion, just as our experience that the "present place" is a point in space is also an illusion. Since all points in time and space are experienced only in this present time and this present point, they are dependent for their existence on the present Now and Here, which in Reality is nothing more than the I AM Presence of our Being. Therefore, our essential Being – I AM – is the sole Reality of not only this present moment and place, but also of the *entire appearance* of time and space.

*****

If what I have shared here has blown your mind and heart open to some degree and, despite any cognitive dissonance you many feel, you intuitively recognize the ring of truth in what I suggest, then I encourage you to try the following contemplative experiment so that this understanding can percolate into your everyday life.

As you go about your day, instead of presuming that the body and world appear "outside" of you, simply presume the opposite – that the body and world appear "inside" you. When you wake up in the morning, take a few moments before you get up to contemplate the inconceivably mysterious possibility that you are not waking up *in* the world, but that your body-mind and the world are waking up *within you*. Then, throughout your day, when you are not otherwise engaged in activities, simply rest as that I AM Presence and *see* that the body, mind and world are a projection and manifestation of your unchanging Consciousness. *Feel* that all beings and things are in essence arising in and as your own boundless Self. *Breathe* the Wide Open Wonder of this astonishing display in all of its multidimensional complexity.

As you give yourself to such contemplation, which is really another form of True Meditation and Wide Open Wonder, your experience of being a human being in the world will become much more dream-like, magical, transparent, free flowing and non-binding. You will find yourself deeply loving other beings and the world, responding ever more creatively and fully to events and situations, yet at the same time you will feel essentially Free from the implication of all that occurs. There is a deepening recognition that because the world of time and space is a projection and manifestation of Consciousness, then all is unfolding as it should, according to an Intelligence that the limited human mind cannot possibly grasp or understand. This dawning realization brings with it the benediction of great peace, even potentially in the midst of tremendous turmoil and suffering.

Another result of this kind of contemplation, is that we start to see that the presumption that all human beings share an independently existing concrete world, and that we are all just tiny insignificant specks made of flesh and thought walking around in it for a limited time, is a very convincing illusion. The illusion is so convincing because in the waking state, we all experience a world that *appears* to have a recognizable shared continuity, unlike our subjective experience in dream. But if we stay with this contemplation of the world appearing inside instead of outside, it may begin to dawn upon us, that the continuity of our shared world appears because we are all "downloading" and projecting variations of the same "program", through the sensory apparatus of our body-minds from Consciousness Itself. Our individual human body-minds have all been "born into" this world-program or realm, within which the unique adventures of countless karmic destinies are playing out yet, at the same time, we are "dreaming" the entire display of manifest existence. It is easy for us to accept that we dream the entire display when we project and experience ourselves as a dream character in a dream world when we dream at night, but what if it is exactly the same phenomenon that is happening in the waking state?

One image that comes to mind to convey this ungraspable Mystery, is that our experience of the world is akin to walking along with a torch on a dark moonless night. Wherever the Light of Consciousness falls, there appears the "world" in that moment, just as a torch illuminates the road we are walking along on a moonless night. The light beam is the static doorway in and through which the changing kaleidoscope of the world appears. All of us, because we have all been born into and are projecting this earthly "world-program", experience a similar world or realm as we navigate through life with our torches. However, none of us ever experience an independently existing concrete world separate from the light beam of our own Consciousness, and what lies beyond the light beam is forever Unknown. And it is not only we human beings in this world-program that experience a shared continuity of conscious experience. Think of an elephant, a worm, a fish or a dog, or a tree or a flower for that matter, these are all forms of Consciousness with their own light beams, and they are obviously experiencing a radically different shared world-program from the one that we inhabit and perceive through our body-mind mechanism and its five senses.

Part of our arrogance as human beings is that we presume that we are in an extraordinary or superior position to know Reality, because we are identified with a more complex blob of meat with a bigger brain, that is using energy in a particular way and that says to itself, "This is Reality." But is that really Reality? At most, it is one angle on it, a particular point of view on it. A more complex, sophisticated point of view perhaps, but still only an angle nonetheless. The elephant, the worm, the dog, the fish, the tree, the flower, and the fly banging its head on the window, all have a different angle on it based on the sensory mechanism with which they are identified. Yet it is the same Reality all the while. Could it be, that your individual body-mind mechanism, is but one portal through which the Great One Consciousness shines amidst multitudes of sentient being-portals, in multitudes of worlds? Ah what an inconceivably mysterious wonder!

# Chapter 33

# On Having No Head

As your attunement and surrender to the Awakening Process deepens, you will find that you are naturally abiding more consistently as the Witnessing Consciousness. Instead of automatically thinking that you *are* your thoughts, feeling that you *are* your feelings and sensing that you *are* your sensations, you more consistently recognize all the changing contents of your experience to be a *relative* expression of who you are, but not *ultimately* who you are.

As your center of gravity shifts from small self to Big Self, from psychological self to Consciousness Itself, from ego "I" to I AM Presence, what you previously presumed to be "subject" – your psychophysical experience of being an individual – is now experienced to be "object". All phenomena that constitute the body, mind and world appear within you, coming and going, but You, as the Witness, are what is described in Hindu Vedanta as "neti neti", which means "not this, not that".

Resting as the Pure Witness, your sense of self widens into a vast Freedom, an expanding ocean of infinite ease and transcendence. Even in the midst of the Great Search, and even when you are caught in the worst of your self-contracting ways, you always have immediate and direct access to the ever-present Witness. You might get fixated for a moment, or many moments, on this or that thought, idea, emotion or activity, but when you fall back into the prior ground of the unchanging I AM, then the whirlpool unwinds and a wider and deeper Ground of Being reveals Itself instantaneously.

Awakening as the Witness breaks the spell of our unconscious identification with phenomenal experience, but there is still further to go in the direct contemplation of Reality. Because we are so conditioned to differentiate the witnessing of things arising (subject) from the things themselves (objects), everything we perceive, from thoughts, emotions and sensations to tree, mountain, flower or star, appears as an object that arises and passes away. As a result of this we almost inevitably conceive of Consciousness as a kind of Absolute Subject, that can be separated out from all the objects that come and go. But when we hold onto nothing, and relinquish even any subtle identification with the Witness, meaning any sense of even a Transcendental "I" that can be separated out from all objects, we fall into a further Revelation about the mystery of Consciousness. In this Revelation the subtle dualism between the world that arises and the Consciousness that perceives it, is penetrated by deeper contemplation of experience.

We usually think of "our" mind as existing "in here" and the world that we perceive through the senses as existing independent of awareness "out there". If you pay close attention right now you will see that you are experiencing the world "out there" as sensations and perceptions. There are visual images, tactile feelings and perhaps sounds, smells, and even tastes if you are chewing or sipping on something as you read this. Where do these sensations arise? Do they arise from "out there"? Or do they arise "in here"? Or would it be more accurate to say that they arise and exist in the Consciousness that transcends and includes the apparent duality of "in here" and "out there"? Is it not true that everything you are conscious of must exist in Consciousness for you to be conscious of it? If you answer yes then ask yourself this question: Is Consciousness something that appears within your experience or is Consciousness the empty, open, dimensionless space that contains all that you are experiencing in every moment?

Look at an object in front of you with an open, relaxed, meditative gaze. It could be your hand, a tree, or a table, whatever is in front of you right now. Just be aware of that object arising in this moment. Then gently let the sense of witnessing the object dissolve into the object itself. Let the object arise in your awareness as if it existed by itself. Allow yourself to become completely *one with* that object, so that "you" do not see it, because "you" do not exist.

As you are looking at that object, becoming one with it, you may notice that you cannot sense your own head. Where you assume your head to be there is instead only that object arising. Now gently release your awareness from that one object, and expand your awareness to encompass everything that is arising in the perceptual field of your Consciousness. Allow yourself to become conscious right now of all that is arising in you. All that you see, all that you hear, all that you touch, all that you smell, all that you taste. Recognize that you cannot find a line of separation between the perceiver and the perceived, realize that the entire world display is arising moment-to-moment right where you once felt your head was.

The British mystic, Douglas Harding, called this the "headless state" in his modern spiritual classic *On Having No Head*. This "open eye meditation", is a very immediate and always accessible doorway to the direct perception of the deepest truth of existence. It simply requires the suspension of the unexamined presumption that there is a subject "in here" and an object or world "out there". When you "suspend" the presumption that you only exist "inside your skin", then it becomes tacitly obvious that whatever you perceive is arising directly on your shoulders, exactly where you presume your head to be. The usual presumed experience of I am "inside my face" in here, and everything else is "outside my face" out there, is undermined and dissolved. Everything that is habitually perceived to be arising "out there" is actually arising "in here", inside your face, on your shoulders where your head used to be! Everything, apparently arising, is occurring in that wide-open Space.

This "headless" unity awareness is not subject or object. It is not split into an "in here" or an "out there". You are literally one with everything that is arising moment to moment. This body is you, everyone is you, the world is you, all of this is you, *is one with you*, is not something which you are in a relationship with, as if you were a "something else". You do not see the mountain or the tree or the stars. You *are* the mountain, the tree and the stars. Hence the knowing and feeling of "you" expands to embrace all Space. All Space is you and everything exists within it. This contemplation exercise has the power to reveal the radical wonder-full Truth that the entire manifest universe is arising within, and as, YOU!

# Chapter 34

# Not One Not Two

Resting in simple, clear, ever-present Consciousness, letting go of all differentiating and interpretative activity of mind, we directly perceive that all the forms that are appearing are vibratory modifications of that Consciousness that we are already are, including all the apparently solid things that we presume to be objective to us. The French mystic and visionary, Teilhard de Chardin, captured this Revelation beautifully when he wrote, "Matter is Spirit moving slowly enough to be seen."

Consciousness Itself is realized to be not merely an Eternal Transcendent Subject, but an All-Inclusive Reality. Then it becomes tacitly obvious that there is no experience of subjectivity that stands apart from objectivity, that there is no subject-object distinction that is ever *literally* true. Subject and object, like time and space, are now seen as being so mutually interdependent that they form an inter-woven continuum, a single unified pattern.

Non-Duality, meaning "not two", is the pure perception that the universe does not exist independent of us, but actually co-arises as we experience it. Suddenly it is obvious that we are not, and never have been, passive experiencers of a Reality that exists independent of our experience of it. Reality has to be experienced to exist. Therefore Reality, Consciousness, God, whatever name we want to give to the indefinable Mystery at the heart of existence, can never be only the experiencer or the experienced alone. Reality always emerges in the interface between the experiencer and the experienced. That, which is experienced, influences the experiencer, and simultaneously the experiencer influences what is experienced.

*****

Let us venture further into this Mystery, right now, very directly in your own experience...

Look down at your body and ask yourself what it is. See that it is only our shared conventions of thought that divide the body into parts like chest, shoulder, arm, wrist, hand and fingers, when in actuality there is only one form that is there. Or look out the window at a tree and see that it is only thought that divides the tree into roots, trunk, branches and leaves, when in actuality there is only one form that is there. Take this investigation further and we see that the names "body" and "tree" are also just concepts that define these forms as discrete things, when in Reality they cannot be separated out from all the other forms that surround them, and nor can they be separated out from you – the Consciousness that perceives them.

A line that creates a boundary between the tree and the earth, for example, is not a true boundary. It is only the mind that divides and separates, while Non-Dual Consciousness joins and unites. In actuality, then boundaries are pure illusions – they "pretend" to separate what is not in fact separable. In this sense, the actual world contains lines that make one form distinct from another, but there are no real solid boundaries. A line or a distinction of difference only becomes a boundary when we imagine that it separates, but does not unite at the same time.

As we release our identification with the filter of the differentiating, labeling mind, it soon becomes obvious that every apparent thing interpenetrates every other thing. Then, we see that this is truly a "uni-verse" – One Song – in which everything is somehow interconnected and unified with everything else. Ultimately there are no independent objects, but rather there is simply form appearing in different patterns and densities, that meld in an intricate web of interrelationship. When we allow the subject-object duality to dissolve, then form *is* Consciousness and Consciousness *is* form. Then the display of creation manifests with a vibrant immediacy that renders everything – a thought, people, trees, stars, even a pile of garbage – into the same Radiance.

Yet while that Radiance infuses all forms equally it does not obliterate the appearance of distinct forms. If we perceive Reality *as it is*, free from the superimposition of mind, every thing shines with the same Brightness, but at the same time each particular form stands out more fully as what it is. Everything is enhanced, vivid, bright and concrete. A leaf, a cloud, a cup, a blade of grass, appears as carving itself out in a very defined delineated way, rather like the images on a high definition TV screen.

What we habitually see, through the re-presentation of mind, is a world of dull familiarity that appears grossly physical and dense. But when our perception is freed from the re-presentation of mind, the world then appears as innately mysterious and full of Light. The conditioned re-presentation of mind *is* the self-contraction, and so when the contraction is released it is literally like we are able to "take in" more Light than we are ordinarily aware of. Letting go of the imposition of mind, is like opening the aperture of a camera lens to flood the film with Light.

As more Conscious Light floods through the body-mind vehicle, every apparent thing that we perceive, from a passing thought, to a cup of tea, a tree or a mountain, is seen to be "not one, not two", and is simultaneously distinctly unique and intrinsically one with all. This pure experiencing is ineffably mysterious, but not in the sense of being vague because, on the contrary, Non-Dual Experiencing is actually very defined and clear. It is only ineffable in the sense that the usual dualistic categories of mind are not operating. The sensation of the breeze, of the earth under our feet, the view of a captivating sunset, the taste of chocolate and the vastness of the ocean, still appear as they did before, but now they are intuitively known and felt intimately as extensions of our own Being.

There are no separate "parts" in the interconnecting wholeness of Consciousness, there is nothing "individual" which stands outside of its inclusiveness. All "parts" which appear to be individuated are multiple extensions of THAT. *Consciousness is the no-thing that gives apparent existence to every-thing.* When the idea of a separate, independent, objective world collapses, so too does the idea of a separate, independent, subjective "I" who is experiencing it. We cannot penetrate further than this. We can only end in the silence of no-thing-ness, drowned in the indefinable Mystery that is Always Already All-That-Is.

This shattering insight is like a light beam of Pure Perception that hits a mirror and then bounces back to completely obliterate the Perceiver. When we let this insight penetrate very deeply we die into the unfathomable Absolute Truth, that *nothing ever happened.* We realize that not only do we not exist as a separate island of thought and flesh, but that we *never* existed, and that the entire convoluted adventure of journeying from the darkness of ignorance to the Light of Non-Dual Revelation has *never actually occurred.* What we have been seeking has always been everything that we see, and that includes us. It becomes absolutely obvious that we can never discover the Absolute Reality as a condition apart from ourselves. The shocking revelation is that not only can we not seek Consciousness, but also that we cannot escape it even for a moment. The all-pervading Consciousness, and that which is aware of itself as "I", are ultimately identical. When we comprehend that our body-mind is an expression of Consciousness Itself, as are all other things, then it is clear that the seeker and the Totality that is sought are already united and always have been.

This is why in Zen Buddhism they call the Revelation of Non-

Duality the "Gateless Gate". From the point of view of the individual seeker, it seems like we have to do something to enter that Non-Dual Consciousness – it seems like we need to pass through a gate. So we meditate, we practice and we contemplate. But when we step through the gate and we turn around and look back, there is no gate whatsoever to be seen, and never has been. We realize that we have never been separate from this Consciousness in the first place, so how could we possibly enter it? When this is clearly recognized, it is clear that Awakening is not a mystical experience, or any kind of "event" that occurs in time. Once we have deeply seen this Truth we will know unequivocally that Awakening has nothing whatsoever to do with any change of state and that there never was anything to seek for. Only then do we come to the *end of all seeking.* The epiphany is a quiet and simple shift in perspective, from the one who is looking for THAT, to the recognition that THAT is already looking.

*****

Yet, when we make that subtle yet profound shift, our experience of individuality is not somehow merged or neutered by this Revelation. The common idea, and expectation, is that our individuality will be united with the greater Consciousness that is exterior to its existence in some kind of blissful, ecstatic fusion. Some people who claim to be Enlightened say that their sense of individuality dissolved, and many spiritual seekers therefore have the expectation that their individual sense of "I" should disappear in the aftermath of an authentic Awakening. But who is it that could say that "my" sense of "I" went away?

Doesn't there still need to be an "I" there to say such a thing?

The truth is that "I" do not go anywhere, all that goes away is what was never really there in the first place, which is the illusion of the *separate* "I". The True "I" casts off this illusion of the separate "I", and yet remains as the "I", such is the Great Paradox of Awakening.

This is an important understanding because it helps us to recognize that once the self-contraction of the ego "I" is released, then the sense of individuality and personality that remains is none other than THAT. The Revelation is simply that there has never been an individual that was separate from the all-pervading Being, Consciousness or God in the first place. Therefore, when we shift into Non-Dual Experiencing, our individuality still exists but there is no longer any exclusive identification with it. We recognize our individual body-mind form as being *distinct* from other forms, but not *separate* from other forms. This is when we realize the true meaning of the word "individuality", which means "indivisible". Then our unique expression as a human being is founded in the Truth of non-separation.

Non-Dual Experiencing reveals that any fixed point of view is ultimately a delusion. Reality is not a fixed something that exists independent of us, it is a fluidity that allows for endless discovery. This open-ended fluidity is the ongoing dance between our individual self-expression and the world. Freed from the constriction of believing ourselves to be static entities living in a static universe, we now live in a wonder-full emergent cosmos that is alive, and arises fresh and new in each moment. We experience our individuality as a dynamic organ of Consciousness, in an open dance with the universe. And, as we dance with the universe, the universe dances with us. And that dance is "not one, not two".

As we dance in the ever-new Revelation of being "not one, not two", and as our Freedom and Happiness expands, we do not really know who is enjoying this Freedom and Happiness, because Freedom is free from the fixed position of a particular self. Yet, we still remain an individual for whom this Freedom and Happiness is relevant, meaningful, lived and enjoyed. We experience and manifest more love, clarity and gratitude. We are simply Free to Be Who We Are. We are Free to be an individual self *and* Consciousness Itself. We are Free to be dual *and* Non-Dual. And we are Free to be not one *and* not two.

# Chapter 35

# Do Here Now

SOME spiritual teachers and seekers say, "Everything is perfect as it is" and some say, "Everything must change". Some say, "We must let our life flow" and some say, "We must change our life now". Followers of the first orientation tend to take the position of *being* over doing. They usually end up *being* spiritual bystanders in relationship to the passing show of life. Followers of the second orientation tend to take the position of *doing* over being. They usually end up *doing* spiritual activism of some kind, getting intensely involved with the passing show of life. But there is a simple, yet profound way to resolve and transcend this seeming paradox of spiritual orientation, this apparent tension between *being* and *doing*. Yes it is true that "everything is perfect as it is", and yes it is true that "everything must change". Yes it is true that "we must let our life flow", and yes it is true that "we must change our life now". The resolution of the paradox is in understanding that our *egoless* impetus to change, both ourselves and the circumstances of life, *is* an aspect of life's flow. Being and doing are not opposites. They only seem to become opposites when we separate ourselves out from life's flow. If we take a fixed position in passive (being) or active (doing), then we have slipped out of the undivided Fullness of our True Nature into a subtle or not-so-subtle dualism.

When we experience the invitation to yield in selfless surrender to Be Here Now, or when we experience the urgency of the selfless impulse to Do Here Now, we are experiencing one side of the same coin of Consciousness Itself. When we truly rest in Being Here Now then, as I described earlier in the book, we undermine the self-possessed strategy of the ego "I", and open the door for the arising of the Power That Knows The Way, that manifests through our inquiry and our actions. When our surrender is profound, at times this Power may surge forth with great intensity and urgency, and then we may find ourselves gloriously overwhelmed by, what I like to call, Pure Passion. By this I do not mean the "red" passion of sexual desire and romanticism but the "white" Passion of the Fire of the Heart. This "white" Pure Passion is not confined to a particular emotion but is the energy of Creation or E-motion – think Energy-in-motion – Itself.

Because most popular spiritual teachings emphasize Be Here Now, or Transcendence, over Do Here Now, or Transformation, many spiritual seekers and teachers alike never truly discover this Pure Passion. If we are fundamentally motivated towards to an inwardly orientated path of escape from the complexity of incarnated existence, then we will most likely get subtly or not-so-subtly trapped in the pristine philosophical beauty of Non-Dual perception and understanding. While we may then have access to the cool, empty expanse of liberated detachment from the contents of Consciousness, we still won't be a fully alive embodiment of That Which Is Uncontainable. We won't be able to live it fully, because living it implies an engagement that is inherently passionate, participatory and transformational. However, if we are willing to let go of all reference points, and even the subtle reference point of "being the Witness", then we will be emboldened to take great risks in relationship to life, and we will progressively unleash our previously untapped capacity for egoless action, that spontaneously expresses this Pure Passion.

Pure Passion is unpremeditated, spontaneous, and intense enlightened action. It is the confrontation and penetration of the relative world by the Absolute energy of the God-Force, of Consciousness Itself. The ecstatic upsurge of Pure Passion propels us toward a dynamic Next, not a static, self-hypnotized, being-in-the-present-moment fixation on the Now. Pure Passion eclipses any dissociative philosophical tendency to withdrawal, that merely witnesses the flow of life at a distance. For Pure Passion says there is not only something to observe, understand and transcend; there is something to be *lived*.

Are you ready to hold onto nothing, and to take the great risk of igniting this Pure Passion? Are you ready to relinquish the dualistic mind, and dive into the ungraspable unity of Be Here Now and Do Here Now? Are you compelled by the possibility of being deeply rested in "no position", while simultaneously being an open conduit for potentially very strong positions to be expressed through you in the world of time and space, as and when that is called for by the ferocity of the Fire of the Heart? Are you willing to jump into that White Fire of Pure Passion with no reference points, awake and available, rooted in Now and ready for Next?

If you are, then you will discover that you are always poised on the edge of Creation. You will discover that in your Awakened surrender to the Non-Dual Reality, you can remain fundamentally Free from the entire passing show of conditional existence, while simultaneously intensely immersed in living participation with it. You will experience the mind-blowing paradoxical truth that ultimately "you", as an individual, are not the doer of action, but rather that action is simply happening through your body-mind as an instrument of a Higher Power. And yet, "you" are also choosing to sacrifice your "self", so that you may become an instrument of that Higher Power. Indeed, it is your intuition of the Divine Reality, here and now, that allows you to live as self-sacrifice, rather than as a narcissistic, reactive and ego-possessed struggle for psychological survival.

If we only orient ourselves to *live* in the Now, then we will eventually find ourselves subtly stuck, usually unwittingly, enjoying the fresh immensity of a bigger view, from what we might imagine to be a metaphorical mountain top, when in reality we have only reached a high plateau. Then we will be aware and awake, but also essentially *aloof*. But if we unselfconsciously *die* to the Now, then we are in free-fall, never settling anywhere, rooted in Now *and* simultaneously reborn for what is Next. Then we will be aware, awake and essentially *available*.

When we let go of holding onto any position in relationship to

Being versus Doing, when we die moment by moment, in heartfelt surrender to the Mystery of Existence, then we become a continuous sacrifice into the Divine Reality. We live in the innocence and Wide Open Wonder of not knowing what the next moment will bring, or what the next moment will call forth from us. In one moment we may find ourselves sitting on a park bench, immersed in the blissful joy of Pure Being, and in another we may find ourselves exploding in a stream of Pure Passion that is shocking in its blazing intensity, and anything else inbetween. Holding onto nothing and leaning into Life, we are free from all confining and defining patterns of self-identity, and in this vulnerable nakedness we meet each moment freshly *as it is*. The moment may manifest as a passing lesson, or as a strenuous Divine Test, or as a blessed benediction in which we are dissolved in utter Mystery and Amazement, merged into the Love-Bliss that is the Source of All. But regardless of how the moment manifests, in the spectrum of experience both high and low, we remain rooted in that mysterious place where the whirlpool of ego has no foothold whatsoever.

# Chapter 36

# The Big Yes

As the Awakening Process unravels the whirlpool of the ego "I", your True Nature as Consciousness Itself shines forth more consistently in both its Witnessing and Non-Dual forms. Sometimes Consciousness is tacitly known as direct unqualified Non-Dual knowing that is Pure Experiencing transcending subjectivity and objectivity; sometimes Consciousness is tacitly known with an accompanying sense of "I" as the Transcendental Witness. Both aspects of Awakened Consciousness have lessons to teach us. Witnessing Consciousness is the vehicle of understanding where all observation, discrimination and reflection take place, and Non-Dual Consciousness is the vehicle of surrender and Pure Experiencing, free from the subject-object duality.

As we rest more and more consistently in these boundless dimensions, concepts like mind and world, inside and outside, personal and impersonal, gradually lose their meaning, because what stands out primarily is simply the all-encompassing actuality of what IS. We still walk and talk and act as individuals, but now we experience a paradoxical sense of simultaneous participation in, and detachment from, the arising field of experience. Thoughts still arise, and actions are done, but the connecting sense of a separate, inner "I", that is the presumed thinker of thoughts, or the presumed doer of action, progressively dissolves.

With this dissolution of the whirlpool of the ego "I", the essential qualities of ever-present Consciousness, such as equanimity, discriminating wisdom and compassion, combine with the native dispositions and particular talents of our unique individual body-mind. We are then motivated, not by the projected promise of the Great Search, but by the liberated intelligence of The Power That Knows The Way. And That Power says a Big Yes to the Wonder of Life that is its own created expression.

When we say Yes to Life with complete faith, trust and surrender, then the qualities and gifts of our own highest potential begin to manifest spontaneously. Those qualities might take the form of compassionate empathy, or discriminating wisdom, or cognitive insight, or artistic creativity, or healing presence, or any other authentic expression in which our humanity is fully realized. Having given up the need to be somebody in particular, having relinquished the attachment to being unique or special, we miraculously discover that the uniqueness of our essential individual self-expression starts shining forth like never before. Everything that we are, and everything we have gone through as an individual – all of our life experience, our learning, all our trials and victories – come to a fruition that is only to be *given*, as our unique offering to the Great Process of Divine Evolution.

*****

Awakening to the Big Yes is an inconceivably delicate and vulnerable opening. We will know this is happening for real, when the pure conscious intelligence that is the source and expression of Life, begins to well up spontaneously and manifest its own True Nature – which is Love. Out of the revelation of Non-Dual Consciousness, the first thing that emerges is spontaneous concern for others and a deep love of the entire display of Creation. This Love, which is wondrous, radiant and inconceivable, can be known only when our striving to grasp and to get for ourselves is transcended.

We could say that this Love accepts everything as Conscious Light, because it transcends and includes the relative polarities of light and darkness. Thus all becomes Light and darkness is dispelled. This is what is meant by the commonly used term, "Unconditional Love". In this way we begin to understand that even all the ignorance, cruelty and injustice in the world, and the suffering we experience when we identify with the self-contraction of the ego "I", is all part of the Light and is embraced by this unfathomable Love. All suffering, pain and horror is contained in God, in Consciousness Itself. And Love is the *felt response* to that suffering, pain and horror. Love feels the wound of separation and ignorance in ourselves and in the world. Love longs to bring the Truth of Prior Unity into manifestation, and yet, paradoxically, at the same time nothing, *literally nothing*, is a problem when we are subsumed in this mind-transcending Love.

We might have a profound and refined understanding of the Absolute Truth of Non-Duality, of "not one, not two", but it is Love, that is the irrefutable proof of it as a lived human expression. This Love far transcends the conventional experience of personal love as a quality of intimacy that characterizes a small circle of relationships or partnerships, connecting one person to another. Rather it is the discovery of an impersonal or universal Love, that is the natural condition of all relationship, of all experience, and therefore is the very essence of Creation itself.

The impersonal, universal Love that shines forth from the Awakened Heart, expresses itself in two distinct yet non-separate expressions. The expression that we most often hear about is experienced as the benediction of "Unconditional Love", which I already mentioned. This Love softens and soaks our entire being with overflowing peace, awe and gratitude for the simple, sweet wonder of being alive. We could say it is the receptive Transcendent pole of Love, that embraces and radically accepts everything *as it is*, and everybody *as they are* as manifestations of Divine Reality. As we gaze upon the vicissitudes of the world, this Love blesses us with a deep unfathomable knowing, beyond the grasp of the mind, that despite war, injustice, cruelty, and so much needless destruction, this Life Process is unfolding as it must. Unconditional Love releases us from the burden of existence, and graces us with the intuitive knowing that all is well. The True Nature of everything and everyone is intuitively perceived and felt to be *always already* rested and washed in One Consciousness.

But then there is another expression of Love that is experienced not as this deep, all-encompassing, healing ocean of peace and acceptance, but as a great burning Fire, that engenders a profound sense of responsibility for the further evolution of the Life Process Itself. It is the penetrative, Transformative pole of Love, that I described earlier, as the "White Fire" of Pure Passion. It can be understood as the human experience of the creative impulse, that is animating and driving the universe. When we experience this Love, our sense of individuality becomes a conduit for that vast unfolding Process that is dynamic and that wants to bring ever-higher orders of harmony and integration into manifestation. This is the movement of what we could call an Evolutionary Love, the purpose of which is to transform manifestation, to transfigure existence, and to glorify Being in form.

*****

I am not using the word "evolutionary" in a scientific sense, that is connected to a particular explanation of the origin of the universe or the biological mutation of species. While modern science provides much useful information about the laws that shape the relative world of nature, its overly materialistic bias means that it has a limited cognitive framework, and so it cannot be unquestioningly trusted as a reliable source of Absolute Truth. Science is ultimately dehumanizing when it is regarded as an absolute philosophical point of view, because it chooses external nature, independent of humanity as the subject of its investigation, and imposes that relative reality as the force that defines us. The physical universe, which science investigates, is only one dimension of a much wider, broader scale of dimensions in which we participate. Because science is based only on observation, and not

on participation, it cannot be fruitfully applied to the inherently relational context of human existence, and nor can it be rightfully applied
to the ultimate context of existence itself. We cannot, by observation
alone, experience that Reality that can only be discovered through
deeply surrendered participation. Thus, adhering to evolutionary theories and narratives, like the Big Bang and the Darwinian mutation of
species, is not synonymous with the felt sense of the spiritual force of
Evolutionary Love that I want to convey. The most sophisticated explanations of today's scientific cosmology may not ultimately be more
accurate than the Adam and Eve creation story in Genesis in the Old
Testament. Indeed, whether human beings are inclined toward devis-
ing elaborate mythic or rational mental explanations of Reality, we
must acknowledge that both orientations are essentially an attempt to
gain control over the Unknowable and Uncontainable Great One – the
Mystery of Existence over which we have no control, and about which
we can have no final knowledge whatsoever.

I am using the term "evolutionary" then, to characterize the felt
experience of a Love in which it becomes clear that individual salvation
in Transcendent Being "beyond the Earth" is not our highest objective.
With Evolutionary Love, the liberation of others is as much our self-
concern – we might almost say it is in our own our Divine self-interest
– as our own Liberation. Liberating ourselves from ensnarement in the
lures of egoic existence in this world – the first Great Search – is our
first victory. And then, to conquer the lure of individual Happiness or
Salvation in a Heaven's Beyond of self-absorbed bliss and escape – the

second Great Search – is the last and greatest victory. Having divested ourselves of all spiritual exclusiveness, our Spiritual Awakening does not only recognize the inherent perfection of everything as it is, but passionately impels us to bring the vision of Non-Dual "Perfection" or "Heaven" to Earth, so that the Absolute Truth of Prior Unity can actually be demonstrated and lived in this relative world of time and space.

Without adhering dogmatically to any particular scientific theory, it is self-evident that the manifest cosmos is dynamically driven to give rise to, what philosopher Alfred North Whitehead called, "the creative advance of novelty". Seen in the light of Non-Dual under-standing, this creative process is the dynamic face of Consciousness, that emerges from timeless Being as a stream or continuum of *coming-into-Being* or *Be-coming.* This is the "Mother Shakti" of Indian spir-ituality that dances the universe into existence. The Cosmic Dance of Mother Shakti is Consciousness revealing Itself as energy, matter and mind, integrating first as atoms, then molecules and cells, that in-terpenetrate and build upon each other, to give birth to a potentially infinite array of complex forms. This creative stream of Conscious-ness, that has given rise to our experience of human embodiment, is now calling upon us, as Awakening human "cells", to break through the centrifugal force of our cellular membrane – the whirlpool of the ego "I" – so that we may not only realize the True Fulfillment of our Individuality, but also *come together* to discover and manifest the potentials of an Awakened Higher "We". I will explore this higher evolutionary potential further in a later chapter called "The Ring of Fire".

When we say an unequivocal YES to this Evolutionary Love, to this White Fire of Pure Passion, it can be experienced as a Great Stream of Consciousness that wells up from the timeless Transcendent Now. Through making ourselves fully available and receptive, our body-mind then becomes a portal or instrument through which the dynamic energy of this creative-advance-into-novelty can burst forth uninhibitedly. When this occurs, we may experience a tangible and ecstatic sense of uplift, a creative and generative movement surging up from within that feels blazingly powerful, intense and urgent.

As we surrender to this Big Yes, we recognize that our human capacity for choice, creativity, inquiry, intuitive wisdom, compassion, indeed all of our unique gifts and positive qualities, reflected through head, heart and hands, are given to us so that we may consciously engage with this miraculous creative Process that has given us form. Then, the gift of our individuality is freed from the limiting illusion of independent self-existence, and transfigured to reflect its true potential as a unique expression of the "Indivisible". Then we understand that the True Fulfillment of our Individuality can only occur when we transcend our identification with, and attachment to, being anyone in particular. When we let go of any vestige of our narcissistic need to be seen as unique or special in our individuality, only then can our True Individuality – our Indivisibleness – fully flower and cast forth its unique fragrance and expression for the sake of the Whole.

# Chapter 37

# Awakening the Dreamer

$A$S WE merge into the deepening intuition and understanding of "not one, not two", we begin to profoundly see and feel that the world is not merely physical in nature, but is in fact *psychophysical*. Matter still appears to be solid and tangible, a shifting kaleidoscope of sights, sounds, tastes, smells, and textures continues to assail us, but now we no longer experience our individuality as a separate, skin-encapsulated island of perception and knowledge standing over and against the appearance of the world. We no longer fundamentally feel ourselves to be a distinct and dissociated experiencer having a procession of experiences. Rather we experience ourselves to be an open-ended dynamic organ of Consciousness, in a creative dance with the cosmos, and as we dance with the cosmos, the cosmos dances with us. Thus, it becomes obvious that the flow of the life of our individual body-mind is not determined by some otherworldly celestial influence or deity, and nor it is determined by vague notions of fate and fortune. Rather we intuitively recognize that we draw into experience the events and relationships that are consistent with our inner nature, and that they are, therefore, the events and relationships that we need to learn and to grow.

*****

When we make the shift from perceiving the world as merely physical to perceiving it as psychophysical, then life is no longer experienced as flowing in front of us on a time scale, from a past to an imagined future via the present moment. Rather the flow of life is experienced as arising from the *inside out.* The conditional appearances of our individual body-mind and the world are experienced as emerging from our innermost depth and expanding out into the apparently outer realm of events and relationships.

As a consequence of this intuited flow, we increasingly perceive of our body-mind individuality, and the appearance of the world, as a realm of *effect* not cause. We recognize that causality is founded not only on the laws of an apparently external nature, but also on what our individual and collective minds superimpose upon the appearance of a world that is none other than the manifest reflection of our own Consciousness. Banished forever is the idea of a Creator God "out there" that set the universe in motion a very long time ago, and looks on from some kind of celestial "control tower" on the edge of the cosmos somewhere. Dissolved forever is any notion that we are victims of circumstance bound to an inexorable wheel of destiny. Rather, we recognize that we, as perceiving and conceiving individual body-minds, have a profound shaping influence on what occurs. Indeed, we are, in large part, the creators of our own destiny, and we are therefore also co-creators of the shared "world program" that all human beings inhabit.

What we most deeply believe, what we most deeply love, what we most deeply fear, flows into the world we perceive and potentially shapes the arising of events. This is because the patterning of our individuated mind and psyche, which is programmed from early childhood with cultural beliefs and definitions, invariably confirms its pre-established tenets. Therefore, whatever we unquestioningly believe in, appears to be real and true. If we believe in God, then there definitely seems to be one, and the believer will see all kinds of "signs" that confirm this belief. If we accept the views of scientific materialism, then the world seems to be obviously impelled by mechanically defined sources and forces. If we believe that luck and fate are forces out there, then they too, definitely appear to be real.

But our beliefs, no matter how apparently accurate and objectively true, never deeply clarify how life really works; they only distort our perception of it to a gross or subtle degree. Thus, the path to greater clarity in relationship to life's unfolding events is not to invent new spiritual-sounding paradigms, like the popular New Age spiritual notion of the "Law of Attraction", but to jettison all the old ones and then see what happens. As we do this through consistent observation, understanding and transcendence of inherited patterns of belief, we will discover that there are always subjective elements to objective patterns we create in life. For example, we may discover that it is our own often unconscious beliefs that invoke our disappointments, our physical ailments, our sense of rejection and fear, etc. We may begin to observe and understand that we attract them via inner conflict and by projecting our own creative power out to illusory forces and sources. If we truly see and deeply acknowledge this truth that the inner effects the outer, then it gradually becomes clear that burning in the Fire of the Heart is not only a scorching ordeal of relinquishing our cherished illusions, but also a potentially jubilant discovery and celebration of fulfilling our individuality and manifesting our purpose and our dreams.

In terms of the law of cause and effect – or karma, as it is called in the East – we will progressively understand that much of our psychological experience and life circumstances in the present are a carryover consequence from a chain of past choices and actions. However, we will also understand that the Freedom, or lack of Freedom, that we experience and demonstrate in relationship to our psychological experience and to the external circumstances of our life in any moment, is entirely our *own choice*. When we most profoundly take responsibility for the radical truth that Freedom is essentially always in our own hands, then we are no longer victims of destiny, no matter how challenging or difficult our circumstances may be. Then we will discover that even the more intractable manifestations of our psychological conditioning, and the more difficult and life-inhibiting circumstances of our lives, *will* gradually begin to change over time, sometimes almost imperceptibly and sometimes quite magically. The reason for this is that the psychological patterning of the body-mind, which "holds" or magnetizes those life circumstances in place, is progressively weakened and undermined, and so there is more "room" for Life, in the form of the creative-advance-into-novelty, to "move". New relationships, opportunities and possibilities have "room" to present themselves, often from "left field" in ways we would never expect. Life opens up in fresh, new and often thrilling ways.

A simple phrase that I love that epitomizes this truth comes from a teacher and friend of mine called Peter Ragnar. He is an extraordinary exemplar of living a life of no limitation, and one of his catch phrases is, "What you set is what you get!" However, he means this in a far more profound sense than the popular "Law of Attraction" New Age slogan. What Peter is pointing to in the simple phrase, "What you set is what you get", is the understanding that deep change for the better can only occur when we Awaken to our True Nature as the *driving force* in the adventure that we call Life. This is the key insight that releases us from the trap of the Matrix, and the psychic straitjacket of the consensus trance of the mind and world, that says the reality of your life is given to you rather than created by you.

Once our centre of gravity has fundamentally shifted from living for "my" life, to living for the sake of Life as a whole, our surrender to the Power That Knows The Way catalyzes the conscious projection of new realities. The notion of "projection" is a popular concept in modern psychology that points to the "blind" projection of one's own negative or positive images and feelings on to other people and events. But when we Awaken to the imperative of Evolutionary Love, and the wild creativity of Pure Passion, a transcendent form of projection, begins to emerge – the conscious and imaginative invention of new futures.

Some may say, "Ah but surely any orientation of energy and attention toward the future must be a creation of the egoic mind, for Truth is only Now." But I say, all thought is not the same. There is the random static of thoughts that arise without any intentionality on our part. There is deductive or discriminative thought devoted to solving a problem or analyzing a situation. There is the repetitious and circular rumination of our narcissistic whirlpool of self-concern. But there is also thought that occurs when one is purposed toward creating something that has *never existed before*. Then the function of mind is freed from the twisted maze of the whirlpool "I" with its endless desiring and fantasizing for self-fulfillment, amidst the shifting kaleidoscope of conditional existence. Then the faculty of mind is harnessed as a *tool* for Consciousness to forge Its creative-advance-into-novelty, through the agency of our individual self-expression. For now we have become an open portal for Life and, having freed ourselves from the life-denying demons of doubt and fear, Life Itself can quicken Its Flow through us.

The universe, in and of itself, does not contain any ultimate lessons about Spiritual Awakening or Enlightenment and how it will be actualized. In and of themselves, all apparent things and happenings in the world are "effects" of the interests of multitudes of seemingly independent living beings. Therefore there is no universal "Great Plan" upon which one can depend, because countless beings of all kinds are thinking, and feeling, and acting, and desiring, and creating innumerable "effects". The teeming totality of all this chaotic desiring and acting is the world that we perceive. So the impact that our Awakening may have on the Whole is something that we must supply. That is up to us. But so far the vast majority of the human race, even those who have embraced the Awakening Process as the ultimate purpose of human incarnation, have generally said no to that. As a race, we have generally opted instead for conformity to various systems that we believe to be external and superior to us. The *always already* Non-Dual Consciousness is *Ultimate* – timeless, dimensionless and without cause – but there are also *no ultimate limits* to the potential creative modifications of that Consciousness. In any arena of life, when it comes to mind, perception, power, empathy, spirituality, and so on, there is always a status quo. And that is the place where an individual or a collective decides, consciously or unconsciously, "Well, that's enough. I'll settle for what I have. I'll stop here." That limit then almost inevitably develops into a largely unconscious subliminal trance that says "Be less than you are, so that we can all come together in a common cause." But this is essentially a twisted doctrine of sacrifice, in which everyone colludes and sacrifices for everyone else, which results in a convoluted mass of denial of True Self. Eventually, this delusion gives birth to an unquestioning dedication to what "everyone else" thinks, and supposes, and assumes, and accepts. The lowest common denominator of consensus in every dimension of life, including spirituality, always implies an absence of creative imagination, passion and risk. Everyone agrees and colludes together to hold a limitation in place that is palatable to the collective, and then gradually over time everyone becomes bored and blindly obedient. But if we are deeply and truly Awakened, meaning not only to the principle of Transcendence but to the principle of Transformation, we will keenly feel the horror of the mediocrity of everyday life, of human beings functioning like cogs in a machine over which they have no control. We will feel that no one in their right senses could possibly do so many of the crazy things that are demanded of us everyday. So then, we will dig deep and tap into previously unknown sources of creative power, we will discover a limitless wellspring of creative imagination, passion and risk that streams up from the roots and is always available, gracing us with the miraculous capacity to always be able to play another card and take the Great Adventure of Life and Consciousness further. Only then, will we realize what audacious courage and humble submission to the White Fire of Pure Passion it takes to pierce the strangling web of despair, defeat and automacy that envelops us as a species. Only then will we authentically BE a Free human being, that does not feel constrained by what already exists and simultaneously makes the as-yet-unborn future real.

*****

When you realize that the world is not merely physical in nature but is *psychophysical* then, from the point of view of your individual body-mind, Reality is a mechanism to manifest your unique purpose. Then you are an enchanter in an enchanted land. You will be able to access the audacity and courage to live your Dream, because you recognize that otherwise you will only partially Awaken, and you will end up "fitting in" to someone else's dream. The deep acknowledgement of this Truth is the discovery that the core process of Reality is *magic*. And magic is not the exception; it is the rule, because "what you set is what you get!" Your visions and dreams progressively become Realized – made real – when you surrender your life to them. When you have the courage to boldly take all of the risks necessary to live your Dream, then life becomes a sacred journey.

The word "calling" is another way to language what I want to convey. The traditional understanding is that we are "called" by something greater than ourselves. To "find one's calling" in the Great Adventure of Life and Consciousness is to finally be able to relax at a very profound level into the very purpose for which we were born, and with which our entire being resonates. What makes a calling truly Spiritual, and different from any calling that the separate ego might experience, is that our primary Calling is from the Divine. Our unique characteristics, gifts and competences are then developed and utilized in service to that primary Calling. For example, we may discover that we are predisposed to be writers, singers, artists, builders or dancers by calling. But what will we write, paint, sing, build or dance as devotees of the Divine? The Divine Itself! The Biblical verse "Do all things as unto the Lord" comes to mind. When our Call, our Dream, is truly aligned with the Fire of the Heart, then we will not only be nurturing and developing our competences and gifts; we will also be placing those competences and gifts in service of the Divine, rather than in service of the purposes of the ego "I".

# Chapter 38

# Pioneers of the Possible

WHAT comes to mind when you hear the word "creativity"? Do you think of the great artistic achievements of Michelangelo or Cezanne, or the literature of Shakespeare or Tolstoy, or musical masterpieces like Beethoven's 9th or Jimi Hendrix's "Are you Experienced", or some other example of artistic, literary or musical genius that you consider truly great? Great feats of artistic creativity are all examples of tremendously creative moments that shape our world, but this is also a tremendously creative moment – right here, right now! There is an inherent creative spark at the core of each and every moment, and within every single drop of experience. Every moment has an element of karma, in the sense of patterns of the previous moment carrying over into the present, so that the manifest world and our familiar physical form and personality continues to exist. And every moment also has a potential element of the creative-advance-into-novelty, that transcends the patterns of the previous moment, so that something new can come into being. In this way, creativity is inextricably woven into the fabric of the universe. So once we have recognized that Life and the appearance of the world is *psychophysical* in nature and

283

we have taken the audacious step of Awakening the Dreamer, then our ability to recognize and participate in the creative openings and opportunities of every moment is ignited and magnified.

This means that we don't need a paintbrush to be creative. Our own unique perspective is our brush. We don't need an instrument to be creative. Our body-mind is our instrument. We don't need a canvas to be creative. Our friends and family and relationships and the unfolding adventure of our life are our canvas. In other words, we don't need to be an artist in the conventional sense to be creative. We just need to be someone who truly wants to Awaken to the sublime beauty and opportunity of each and every moment. Then we will become an artist of Life, regardless of our particular skills or talents or styles of self-expression.

When you Awaken the Dreamer, you will become a Pioneer of the Possible, and you will discover where your energy is drawn creatively. When you discover where your energy is drawn creatively, you will also discover that you are a genius at it. And when you discover what your Dream is, then you must give yourself to it with the White Fire of Pure Passion. In so doing you will transcend yourself in it and you will be in service to the Divine.

When the self-serving agenda of the separate ego is fundamentally broken, then what we are living for are not our personal tendencies, and the development of our competences and talents, for the purpose of seeking our own fulfillment. Rather we find ourselves living for universal creative themes and open-ended possibilities that far transcend the sphere of conventional existence as it is commonly lived. The power of our Dream, of our Calling, in whichever way it uniquely manifests, will then impact others and the world most profoundly. Our individual self-expression then becomes a pioneering portal for a higher order of life-affirming, sensitivity and intelligence appearing in human form.

To Awaken to the radical insight that you *are* the Dreamer, that you *are* the Call, that you *are* the Creator, is to be fully and vibrantly alive, and to live gloriously overwhelmed by life's limitless possibilities. You are no longer waiting for the experience of life to become complete. You come down to earth to ecstatically mingle with humankind, the animals, the trees, the elements, and the seething kaleidoscope of phenomena. You lose yourself in the multitudinous display of the world and, wherever your eyes fall, and with every step you take, there you find your Self.

When you realize that anything is possible then the way that you respond to life begins to break boundaries. All that was fixed and known is exploded, as that which was previously unconceivable becomes manifest. You find yourself living in a state of more or less constant amazement and revolution; dying every day by holding onto nothing, and living every day on the edge of the possible. Merged in the ungraspable paradox of Be Here Now and Do Here Now, of the burning brightness of the Fire of the Heart, you discover a courageous willingness to make a continuous leap into the Unknown that creates a completely new evolutionary context for human life.

\*\*\*\*\*

What I am describing here is a profound Creative Process that is not a snap-of-the-fingers "New Age" trick of manifestation; it is a life radically and FULLY lived. While it is conceivable, if more and more individuals become so Awakened, that this Process may belong to the further evolution of humanity as a whole (assuming that we do not destroy ourselves in the meantime), truly living as the White Fire of Pure Passion will never be an everybody-all-at-once mass movement of Awakening. The evolutionary law is that it is always the Pioneers of the Possible who are the growing tip of Consciousness, manifesting new potentialities in the dance of Creation. It is the ones who are mad to live, mad to create, who can and will never settle for the yawn of mediocrity and smug glow of self-satisfaction, that break new ground and lay down the tracks for others to follow. Therefore, it is always a new and unique road for each courageous Awakened Individual. This is why, if you have the courage to live a life of such radical and pioneering surrender, your joy and ecstasy will also be punctuated and tested at times by periods of persistent frustration and immense challenge. This is inevitable, because the current "operating system" of the human race has little to do with the ultimate Truth of Existence. The Awakening Process is still in its infancy on any significant collective scale because the vast majority of humanity is still dependent, still violent, still self-serving, still seeking for consolation and fulfillment in the realm of changes. So do not imagine for a moment that it is an easy matter. It is the Great Work of Divine Evolution Itself. It is a sacred obligation, and you cannot enter into it casually. If you truly allow your life to burn up in the Fire of the Heart, you must expect to be increasingly at odds with the conventions and values of ordinary life, because every aspect of who you are is being transfigured to create and sustain a different purpose and pattern. If you are going to truly embody the radical truth of Spiritual Freedom in this world, then the status quo will not be able to contain your revolutionary Spirit. And so you must be ready to confront enormous opposition. You must be ready to bear the arrows in your back. You must be resolute and deeply committed like a strong tree that cannot be moved, so that you will always emerge victorious from the Divine Tests and Dark Nights.

Despite the never-ending frustrations and challenges involved, it is essential to understand that your Liberation is not dependent upon your Dream or Calling achieving any particular result in time and space. For as long as you are given over wholeheartedly to manifesting your Dream, to embodying your Calling, without reservation, without holding anything back, you *are* intrinsically Free, and then your legacy to this conditional realm will be what it will be. Burning in the Fire of the Heart is not about living primarily *for* conditional existence, it is about living freely and creatively *within* the theatre of conditional existence. It is about understanding and going beyond what you are inclined to do by egoic tendency, so that all your doings are about Freedom Itself and the Realization of What Is Great.

*****

While there are all kinds of ways in which human beings have evolved over millennia, and there are also all kinds of ways in which we can improve our current world-situation, the humanly perceived world has essentially always been groaning under the same weight of human ignorance. That fundamental "suffering", in the sense that Gautama Buddha meant it when he declared the tenet "Life is suffering" to be the foundation of his teaching, is the nature of mortality and conditional existence itself. And so it is with human life, human history, human experiencing, and all conditional existence that we experience in the waking state. Everything is constantly changing, and while there may be all kinds of relative changes for the better in socio-political functioning, it doesn't necessarily get any better in fundamental terms, and it simply cannot unless there is a wider movement of True Spiritual Awakening that goes far beyond the personal orientation to life. Despite the arising of the great World Religions and the appearance of numerous extraordinarily Enlightened Spiritual Masters, and despite the ever increasing evidence of the devastating consequences of war, ecological collapse, and the addictive cycles of consumption that fuel the Great Search, our essential ignorance, our self-centeredness, our narcissistic infatuation with the hypnotic whirlpool of our ever shifting fears and desires, has hardly changed collectively at all. In fact, in the spiritual wasteland of Western culture, that is rapidly colonizing the known world, it has clearly gotten worse.

Many factors are causing the historically unique confluence of global crises that are overwhelming humanity at the present time, particularly the ever-widening gap between the immensely powerful few and the majority who still struggle for survival, and our burgeoning technological capacities, that far outstrip our moral and spiritual development as a species. And so now we live in a time in which there are many signs that even the entire world, the Earth itself, could be destroyed or made uninhabitable. But it is interesting to question, how different this is from hundreds or thousands of years ago, when people thought the limit of the world was the tree at the edge of the village, or the mountain range in the distance, or the horizon of the ocean, and they feared that their village, nation or civilization was threatened. For them it was the confrontation with the end of the existing world, just as it is for us today. This is not to say that our current confrontation is not more urgent and real in its implications, in the interconnected world of today, rather what I am pointing to is that this human dilemma of confronting the existential "end of history" has always been an aspect of mortal human existence. The White Fire that I am attempting to describe is not dampened by such potential endings, and nor is it dependent on any phenomenal beginnings for its ignition. No matter what stage of historical evolution or devolution, no matter the social conditions, no matter the climate, no matter whether there is peace or war, there is always and only the struggle of the Individual, his victory or defeat, his liberation or enslavement. It is this endeavor of Awakening to, and as, the Fire of the Heart, that is the cosmic Purpose of our individual and shared existence. And that Purpose transcends, and ultimately defies all analysis, whether scientific, political, philosophical or even spiritual.

So as we Awaken to the ecstatic surge of Pure Passion, of Evolutionary Love, that calls us to give creative expression to our Dream, it is essential that we remain grounded in, and surrendered to, the Principle of Consciousness, that always *transcends and includes* the principle of Life, and the principle of light versus darkness. The Principle of Consciousness defies description, and It is not an extension of the world or of any convention of knowledge. It is the Absolute Conscious Light that *transcends and includes* the duality of light versus darkness, of good versus evil. So that is why we must always resort with heartfelt devotion to True Meditation, to Wide Open Wonder, to the White Fire of the Power That Knows The Way, to the Indivisible Ground of what Gautama Buddha called "Right View", that *always already* transcends the "point of view" of the separate self. Then, even in the face of unbearable desecration, destruction and darkness, and as we steadfastly devote our blood, sweat and tears to the actualization of our Dream, we will forever find ourselves *always already* Home.

# Chapter 39

# The White Radiance
# of Eternity

THE ROMANTIC poet Percy Bysshe Shelley, while meditating on the meaning of life and death, after the untimely death of fellow Romantic poet John Keats, wrote in his beautiful poem Adonais;

*Life, like a dome of many-coloured glass,*
*Stains the white radiance of Eternity,*
*Until Death tramples it to fragments. – Die,*
*If thou wouldst be with that which thou dost seek!*

Shelley's metaphor, which comes from the imagery of stained glass as found in European Christian churches and cathedrals, is a perfect one to illustrate how the apparent divisibility and duality of the world – the "dome of many-coloured glass" – is due to a fracturing of the Absolute Conscious Light that shines through it. This apparent fracturing, or "staining" of the "white radiance of Eternity" by Life's "dome of many-coloured glass", produces all the apparently separate and discrete objects we see, touch, hear, smell and taste. But this fracturing or "staining" is revealed in Death to be an apparition, to be an appearance that is not *ultimately* Real. Death "tramples it to fragments", revealing that the "dome of many-coloured glass" does not change or diminish the essence of the Light in and of Itself.

Shelley's extortion to, "Die, If thou wouldst be with that which thou dost seek!", points not only to physical death, but to the potential spiritual death of authentic Awakening, that graces us with the Revelation of the "white radiance of Eternity" while we are still embodied as individuated body-minds, appearing within the "dome of many-coloured glass". We must die and be reborn, we must die to the flesh and be reborn as Spirit. This is why Jesus said, "Except a man be born again, he cannot see the Kingdom of God". The need for us to sacrifice our individuality, in order to be born anew as Spirit, is a recurring theme in the teachings of Jesus, "He that seeks to save his life shall lose it and he who loses his life for My Sake shall find it".

When we die to the separate ego "I", even momentarily, we realize that the experience of Life doesn't truly *stain* the "white radiance of Eternity", rather all experience is a temporary modulation of that Radiance that never changes. No experience, no colour, and no stain, can leave a trace upon the Conscious Light that includes and transcends All. That Conscious Light – the white radiance of Eternity – cannot be modified, enhanced or destroyed by any experience whatsoever. It is that Conscious Light that shines within all of us as the knowledge "I AM", and this I AM Presence is the irreducible element in all experience, as light is the irreducible element of all colour.

*****

In order to know and experience anything at all the dimensionless, infinite field of Conscious Light must assume a location or "point" from which it can view, know or perceive experience. It is our individual body-mind that is that location or point of view. The individual body-mind is a mechanism or agency through which the indivisible Conscious Light locates, and thus appears to limit itself, by seeming to become a separate subject of experience.

That separate subjective point of view is the action of attention itself operating through the faculties of mind and the five senses. And that act of attention is the fracturing or "staining" of the "white radiance of Eternity", or the indivisible Conscious Light. Yet despite that fracturing or "staining", which gives rise to the appearance of duality, the Conscious Light Itself is *always already shining*. The relative appearance of the world – the "dome of many-coloured Glass" – is arising within and permeated by its Radiance. The Light Itself experiences no difference. It is only our exclusive identification with a self-contracted, separate, subjective point of view that appears to "stain" or "filter out" the "white radiance of Eternity", or the Absolute Conscious Light, that is our True and Ultimate Nature.

We can better understand this fracturing act of attention by visualizing the appearance of the body, mind and world as a vast electronic field. Imagine a television with a picture formed by a myriad of pixelated electronic dots. Now expand out from a two-dimensional screen to a three-dimensional realm with an infinite number of electronic dots. Your individuated point of view is one dot in one position in this moment, and in the next moment it will be in another position. Attention can move to any one of those dots instantaneously, without moving through everything in between. Attention is the point of awareness – "your" point of view – that arises in conjunction with a great electronic medium, that has the capacity to represent itself as apparently solid matter, subtle form and energetic phenomena or just light, or darkness, or nothingness.

Through practicing True Meditation, and dying into the disposition of Wide Open Wonder, our outwardly directed energy and attention is gradually or suddenly released from its preoccupation with, and bondage to, the infinite field of dots. In that release, if it is profound, we spontaneously Awaken to the always already Transcendent Field of Conscious Light, in which this mechanical act of attention is being moved. Then, whenever attention does move, wherever it moves, its objects are inherently, instantly recognized as modifications of that Conscious Light. They are still what they are as an appearance, but now they are recognizable in their Source Condition. As Teilhard de Chardin said, "Matter is Spirit moving slowly enough to be seen".

Throughout the Awakening Process it is not the faculty of attention itself that changes. Without that faculty our individual body-mind, and the world it perceives, could not appear, and also our body-mind could not function and navigate through this world of changes. What Gautama Buddha called "Right View" then, is not the view of attention itself. "Right View" is when attention is understood to be secondary to the Principle of Consciousness Itself, which transcends and includes all the dots appearing in the three-dimensional electronic field. All objects, all opposites and all points of view are transcended and included in the limitless, dimensionless ISness of Conscious Light. With that transformation of view, the objects perceived and the movement of attention are still experienced, but they are no longer experienced as *binding*. This transformation of view is what we experience as soon as we stop holding ourselves to only one spot in Consciousness. Then there is no self-contraction as an egoic reaction in the midst of conditions. All appearances are understood to be kaleidoscopic ephemeral apparitions, or modifications of Conscious Light, that are relatively real, but not *ultimately* Real.

So then we may well ask, "Why is this all happening? What is the Purpose of it all? Why is this entire display even occurring?" But this question cannot *really* be answered. I could try to give you a somewhat satisfying philosophical answer like: "God wanted to experience consciously Awakening to Himself in form. So first He forgot Himself, and then, through a few sensitive souls, Awakened to Himself again, and undertook the Process of Consciously Realizing Himself in and as the world of form..." Something like that may be a somewhat satisfying answer intellectually and even intuitively, but it doesn't address the fact that we are asking the question from the point of view of *already presuming* ourselves to be separate. In asking such a question we presume that separation has *already* occurred, and that it has occurred in the form in which we perceive it to exist. However, the Revelation of Reality or Conscious Light Itself, is radically Free from the presumption of separateness. The Reality of Conscious Light doesn't have to account for the illusion that we are suffering from. Therefore, when we are asking, "What's the purpose of it all?", we are asking about our own illusion of reality that issues from our own point of view, due to our apparent association with a mortal body-mind organism.

It is interesting to consider that all the existential questions that ask "Why?", usually come from a presumption that something is wrong or missing; for example: "Why am I here?", "Why is all this happening?", "Why is there evil and suffering in the world", "Why did God create the ego?"... But the Truth is that there is nothing wrong with the cosmos *as it is*. The cosmos is a manifest reflection of Consciousness, Spirit, God, the Supreme Identity. It doesn't require a purpose, because our suffering, our anguish, and our relentless need to know *don't come from there*. All of that is something that we are *superimposing* on this appearance. It is something we are doing out of our own fear.

*****

Consciousness, Spirit, God, the Supreme Identity, is alive as everything that appears and disappears, including all of us. We are either contracting in fear, binding ourselves to what appears – friends, lovers, children, house, work, money, our body, our thoughts, building up a historical sense of self, a whole inner world of comfort, ideas and hopes for the future – or we are surrendering it all in every moment, loving completely and letting go completely, trusting life and the Fire of the Heart to live us and the unfolding adventure of our lives.

Attention or point of view still persists as the principle whereby the apparition of duality is made possible, and through which we are able to walk and talk as an individual in the world, but every moment that we resort to this radical understanding that There Is Only God, the root of our separate, personal point of view is undermined. The imaginary locus at the center of the whirlpool of the ego "I" is dissolved, is subsumed, and is sublimed, into the vast, uncontainable incomprehensibility of the Ocean Itself.

A life lived in consistent surrender to the sublimity of that Ocean, to the ungraspable "white radiance of Eternity", is always already a movement in Eternal Sunlight. Clouds and storms may apparently obscure and "stain" the perception of the Sun's Light, but we are always wedded to, and infused by, the Source Itself – the Sun.

As true devotees of this glorious Transcendent Truth, we are eternally and immeasurably gifted, blessed, unbounded, undefined and radically and ecstatically Free...

*Cosmic Dancers and Dreamers*
*Dancing and dreaming*
*In the midst of the highs and the lows*
*And the nights of dreadful darkness*
*And the days of honeyed light.*
*Crossing the twilight of illusion*

*Sun-eyed children of a marvelous dawn*

*Creators of What Is Great*

*With wide brows of Calm*

*Breaking the barriers of the world*

# Chapter 40

# Ring of Fire

W HEN our life becomes a movement in Eternal Sunlight, when Evolutionary Love lights us up, then our orientation to the Awakening Process completely transcends the notion of "my" Spiritual Awakening. With our energy and attention liberated from the whirlpool of narcissistic self-concern, even from concern for our own Enlightenment, we feel more and more compelled by the longing to come together with other Awakening human beings. This is because Evolutionary Love calls us to the Realization that we are relational beings, whose existence can never be separated from the existence of others, and from the entire universe. It becomes self-evident that we co-exist, not as individuals living side by side, but as part of a matrix of relatedness from which we are never separate. When the Pure Passion of Evolutionary Love ignites in the hearts and minds of a group of people, it is that matrix of relatedness itself that longs to consciously Awaken and Evolve, as a collective expression of the One in the Many.

What would human life and culture look like if we fully opened ourselves to this White Fire of Pure Passion, this Evolutionary Love? Having freed ourselves from the mythic dogmatisms of traditional religion, having transcended the disenchantment and materialistic bias of the modern rational mind, and having liberated ourselves from the narcissistic self-absorptions of postmodernity, what kind of new world could human beings aligned with the trajectory of the Fire of the Heart actually express and create?

In the earlier chapter called "The Big Yes", I explored how the trajectory of the Fire of the Heart emerges from timeless Being as a stream or continuum of coming-into-Being or Be-coming. Looked at through the lens of an evolutionary perspective, informed by some of the key insights of Western science, this continuum of Becoming reveals a pattern of progressive integration as atoms, then molecules, and then cells, transcend and include each other to give birth to a potentially infinite array of complex life forms.

One interesting way to frame our experience of human incarnation is that we are an extraordinarily complex "cell", that has transcended and included what came before in the evolutionary unfolding from energy to matter to life to mind. Our Spiritual Awakening can be likened to a piercing of the membrane of that cell. Then the energy and intelligence that created our individuated cell is liberated and made available for its next creative-advance-into-novelty. Once this piercing, this Awakening, has occurred to the degree that we cannot go back to being the isolated "cell" of skin and thought that we presumed that we were before, we will feel the magnetic pull to come together with other Awakening human "cells". The reason for this is that the self-transcending drive of the Awakening Process is not only purposed to the Realization of the True Fulfillment of our Individuality, but also to the Realization of the True Fulfillment of an Awakened Higher "We". When we break through the centrifugal force of our individual cellular membrane – which is synonymous with the whirlpool of the ego "I" – then we make ourselves available for the potentiality of a *Collective Emergence*, that transcends and includes our individuality.

India's great evolutionary mystic Sri Aurobindo, believed that humanity was a "transitional species", and he envisioned a leap in human evolution that would surpass human mentality and give birth to what he called the Supermind and the Superhuman. This is what he had to say about the potential of an enlightened collective;

> *In the actual state of humanity, it is the individual who must climb to this height as a pioneer and precursor. But if a collectivity or group could be formed of those who had reached the supra-mental perfection, there indeed some divine creation could take shape; a new earth could descend that would be a new heaven, a world of supra-mental light could be created here amidst the receding darkness of this terrestrial ignorance.*

Whether what Aurobindo envisioned is a true harbinger of what may be possible in terms of human evolution or not, I have no doubt that when we truly Awaken to the White Fire of Pure Passion, we will recognize that the entire process of cosmic evolution is a Singular Intelligence, and that we are all potentially a unique expression of the creative-advance-into-novelty. And when we come together with others in whom that White Fire has also been Awakened, then we will have harnessed the potential to enter into, and create, a new Awakened culture and world *together* sourced in the Spiritual Ground of Prior Unity.

The Awakened "Higher We" opens up when the Absolute Truth of Non-Dual Consciousness comes alive between subjects. This happens when it becomes tacitly and instantly obvious that there is only One Being animating our unique forms and shining through our many eyes. Then we Awaken to a collective field, in and between us, that is Self-Aware. That Collective Awakened Being is pregnant with the undeniable sense of the Sacred, and is felt to be inconceivably delicate in its freshness and newness.

I spent many years involved in a very dedicated spiritual community called EnlightenNext, that came together in the sacred pursuit of a new way of being human, and it was largely devoted to exploring and catalyzing this Collective Awakening. It was a volatile and innovative experiment, that was both truly inspired and groundbreaking in radical ways, and also dysfunctional and destructive in other ways. However, despite the mistakes and shadows that were a part of that Play, the best of what came out of it was truly extraordinary, and catapulted many of us who were involved far beyond what we ever thought was possible. During those times, I was graced with many radical and profound Awakenings, and I was also blessed to be a part of some monumental spiritual breakthroughs in Collective Awakening. To best illuminate the collective potentials that I have known and seen with my own Heart, I am going to share an article I wrote about an event of Collective Awakening that occurred in 2001.

To introduce this article it is important to understand that many years of individual and collective practice, which included meditation practice and group inquiry sessions, formed the context for this event. Those sustained years of practice created a profound Ground of Freedom, and an unusual depth of trust and intimacy, between all involved. This event was also preceded by what I can only describe as a "Collective Dark Night of the Soul", during which all of us involved were confronted with an onslaught of egoic rebellion that was unprecedented in our experience until that point. As I understand it now, the primary reason why our individual and collective resistance was so extreme was because we were pushing for an actualized breakthrough into a *collective* matrix of Awakened Consciousness beyond ego. This was not the "Enlightenment" of the great traditions, with the goal of transcendence of the world, and nor was it a potential that could be known and expressed by one even extraordinarily enlightened individual alone. What we were endeavoring to bring into being was a literal mutation in our shared humanity, a mutation that far transcended anything that we could "have" for ourselves, or even understand with that rather limited apparatus called "mind". Thus, the force of resistance that asserted itself within us, had its roots in deep structures of self-preservation that went far beyond any of us personally. We were confronting the impersonal forces in the human condition, that were inconsistent with the deepest truth of our Being, that now longed to be born in an unprecedented new form. We were forging a new pathway for the evolution of consciousness, and we were the vehicles for this mutation.

The stakes were very high and for a long time during this Dark Night there did not seem to be any light at the end of the tunnel. There were junctures were it appeared that our evolutionary experiment might ultimately fail, that Heaven had slipped from our grasp, and many of us sank into caverns of despair and numb indifference that were quite simply Hell on Earth, and still make me shudder whenever I recall them. Whether we knew it or not we were all cells in a greater organism, that was going through an evolutionary metamorphosis.

As we emerged one by one from that Dark Night, in which we had undergone an intense period of purifying burning in the Fire of the Heart, we began to meet in a circle regularly to explore and give voice to what was opening up. There were a series of meetings that led up to the meeting I am going to describe. In those meetings some individuals in the group had accessed and stabilized in a ground of profound Awakening, and their transmission of that Absolute Consciousness exerted an electrifying evolutionary tension upon everyone else to meet them in that Revelation. Through taking an ongoing absolute stand with all the movements and motivations in themselves that were rooted in the separate ego, they found ourselves coming together in the surging knowledge of their True Identity as One Self like never before. It was astonishing to witness, as spiritual brothers I knew so well were clearly radically transformed. The past had literally fallen away. They were all expressing an authentic doubtlessness, a liberated passionate care and a penetrating subtlety of discrimination that was remarkable and breathtaking. Many of us struggled to meet this challenge, as nothing less than a genuine heartfelt authentic response could match the searing singularity of the Awakened Consciousness that reigned in the room. The degree of subtlety with which any trace of impurity was being recognized and illuminated was absolutely challenging and unthinkably profound. With each meeting the stakes rose, and the noose tightened around any attachment any of us had to expressing ego in any shape or form. Whether it was expressed as a victimized relationship to our past or our conditioning, fear of letting go of our defenses, some degree of arrogant over-confidence and self-satisfaction, or an unwillingness to trust in others and fully participate, the movement of the separate ego was seen and named for what it was – the impersonal force within that had to be transcended for the sake of a higher emergence. The circle burned with a sacrificial fire. There was no way back or around this demand. One could cut the evolutionary tension in the air with a knife. Over the course of the meetings, one man after another relinquished their fear, pride, doubt and hesitation, and in the moment of that letting go jumped into the Fire that was burning in the centre of the circle. The meeting I am going to describe occurred when the last man let go completely...

*From the very beginning each individual spoke with a pure passion, disarming transparency and resolute authenticity, that expressed only their highest and deepest experience.*

*As the last man who was still holding on to a vestige of doubt let go in an ecstatic expression of release, the circle exploded into a Ring of Spiritual Fire, as we found ourselves consumed and transported beyond all knowing into the uncontainable mystery of a collective enlightened Consciousness.*

*All distinctions between the One and the Many rapidly dissolved in a searing conflagration of Unity. Every individual – mysteriously more fully themselves than ever before – melted into a glowing field of luminous energy. There was only One Heart, One Mind, and One Voice that hungered to speak. But what was so new and utterly awe-inspiring was the unmistakable Presence of a Greater and Higher Intelligence, that was emerging in this context of a seamless blend of autonomy and communion.*

*This Revelation was far more than a spiritual experience. It was the palpable sensation of becoming a conscious part of an even more infinitely conscious Whole. It was as if we had somehow forged ourselves into a Great Unified Receiver, that was now able to pick up a signal that had always been there, but had hitherto been beyond our reach. A new matrix of Awakened Consciousness, literally a new Being, unshackled from any vestige of separation, was surging into manifestation through us and as us.*

*As each man abandoned himself without reservation and*

*gave voice to his deepest heartfelt intuitive recognition of what was being revealed, the Ring of Fire vibrated with a luminous insistent call, that seemed to erupt from the depths of our souls, and from the infinite vastness of the overarching cosmos simultaneously. This newly liberated collective Intelligence had its own agenda, and was pregnant with a purpose that held the fruition and resolution of the human predicament within it. We tacitly and simultaneously knew this potential was utterly real, and miraculously we were able to express it.*

*As each man leaned into the Ring of Fire, the more the Whole Collective Field Awakened to Itself, and the more it became clear that each of our individual self-expressions were becoming a cell within a Greater Being. We were both at the center of the Whole Field, and a unique organ of perception simultaneously. We were both part and whole together.*

*One after another we gave voice to our recognition that this Collective Emergence revealed the potential for not only the end of all conflict, but the creation of a new order of human relationship and a new world. A new epoch of limitless possibility was dawning and breaking over us in ecstatic waves of Revelation. We spoke of the sensation of standing on the threshold of a new understanding of human existence, peering into our collective evolutionary future – the status quo of separation and conflict superseded by a miraculous context of unity and resounding creative purpose. We had miraculously penetrated together to the very fount of Creation, and we were being called to be its servants. In light of this we knew nothing could ever be the same again, and the implications of what we were here to bring into manifestation were far beyond what we had ever considered possible.*

*The meeting came to a seamless and unmistakable close as the words of the last man to speak trailed off into an immensely palpable Silence, and the Ring of Fire of that Transcendent Higher Intelligence seemed to spiral upward and out of the room. We sat gazing across the circle at each other, absolutely stunned in silent awe. Drenched in a Love that knew no bounds, we had been emptied of all self-importance.*

When I look back on it now, the explosion that began on that night, and that continued to flare forth unabated like an erupting volcano over several weeks, was a collective initiation into a new matrix of human potential. It was as if a rocket had finally achieved "escape velocity", and broken through the gravitational field of the collective postmodern ego, and suddenly a new orbit or higher octave of Spiritual Power and Intelligence was miraculously available to those with the necessary integrity of interest, passion and receptivity.

What was, and is, so remarkable about this phenomenon is that the power of illumination and insight revealed in such a Collective Awakening is not accessible by an individual alone, even if they have been repeatedly immersed in such events. When each individual involved is consumed by that Ring of Fire, what they give voice to is their own unique self-expression, but at the same time, it is tacitly obvious that nothing that is being expressed is sourced in any individual. Another remarkable feature of this phenomenon is that if this Ring of Fire is repeatedly catalyzed and engaged with the same individuals over time, the experience of "reactivating" it clearly evolves. A seemingly never-ending cascade of new insights and understandings is always available, that potentially build on what came before. It is as if the Collective Awakened Being, the greater organism that is made up of the individual Awakened cells, has a Life of its own and experiences a searing Pure Passion to explore Itself through the shared inquiry.

It is important to appreciate and understand that what I am attempting to describe is very rare. It is not just a group of people being ecstatically inspired together, and through that creating a spiritually charged atmosphere in the room. What I have attempted to describe is far more profound and has far greater implications. These higher levels of Consciousness potential, that can be made manifest through Awakening human beings, are not pre-existing structures existing somewhere in the metaphysical "ether" waiting for all and sundry to stumble upon them. It takes true Pioneers of the Possible, and an extremely dedicated effort to discover, explore and create them. It takes some fearless people who explore the boundaries of their own ability to expand beyond their small egoic selves, and who, inspired by a deeply spiritual identification of their individuated, creative selves with the Absolute, put themselves in service of higher levels of Being in a direct, uninhibited expression of the God-Impulse. The phenomenon of the Ring of Fire can only occur when everyone involved has completely relinquished their attachment to, and fascination with, any self-referential thought or emotion. Only when the individuated whirlpools have all unwound, and turned their hearts out to the Great Ocean, or Heart that is the Context and Source of All, can the whole group become aware of, and a conduit for, the Spirit Current of Awakening in the Collective.

Awakening to this Collective Spirit Current, this New Being, has tremendous implications for all of us as a race, for in this Recognition-Response, something infinitely greater than the mode of humanity we are presently experiencing is longing to be born. If we are blessed with the opportunity to come together with others in True Spiritual Communion, if we are willing to make ourselves available to this New Being, if we take the risk to allow It to express Itself through our individual and shared lives, we will find ourselves knowing things we could never have known before. We will find ourselves daring to do and say things we could never do or say before. We will rediscover our brightened humanity experiencing Reality in ways that we could never have imagined or experienced before. Our body, mind and life will be infused with the all-embracing Consciousness and Delight of the Absolute. We will not only know ourselves as an infinite ego-transcending Consciousness *beyond* all change in time and space, but we will also become *one with* all the outpouring of Consciousness *in* time and space. We will become capable not only of deep peace and equanimity, but also of free and infinite delight in Existence.

The individual life, mind and body that we transcend in Being, will be transfigured and infused with the true Becoming of the Great One, but no longer in the modality of a purely individual narrowness. Our experience of the life force, that animates our individuality, will no longer be experienced as an egoistical activity of sensation and desire, but as a free movement of Universal Life. Our experience of mind will not be of a separate mentality, but rather a larger movement and aspect of Universal Intelligence. Our experience of our emotional, feeling nature will be widened and magnified into a deeply vulnerable and boundless Love, radically free from all contraction, that releases tremendous force and energy. And we will be amazed and filled with awe, in heartbroken devotion and surrender to the Great One, as we are literally forged and transfigured into the instruments through which the Divine Reality of Conscious Light can manifest in a form that is unprecedented in this world.

# Chapter 41

# Extra-Ordinary

I OFTEN say that to authentically live the spiritual life is to become more and more extra-ordinary. The dual meaning of this word – extraordinary and extra-ordinary – captures another paradox at the heart of the Awakening Process. When we begin to consciously engage a spiritual path, we are captivated by the promise of the extraordinary. For example, the notion of abandoning everything and going to India is an idea that commonly fascinates people who have heard a little about spiritual things. The popular images of spiritual life tend to idealize spiritual attainment as some kind of more or less constant experience of blissful ecstasy, of subtle visionary phenomena, of superhuman powers, in the context of a life lived in a disposition of fundamental relinquishment of all the ordinary and mundane responsibilities of life.

As I described earlier, the search for the extraordinary, and the attachment to the subtle phenomena of "spiritual" experience, is in essence no different from any other addiction. As long as we persist in the orientation of spiritual materialism, meaning that we equate Awakening with some particular experiential extrasensory or feeling quality, we will create and feed the very convincing illusion that so many spiritual seekers labor under; namely the apparent "gap" between my "extraordinary" spiritual life and my "extra-ordinary" everyday life.

When most of us turn to spiritual life we seek what is extraordinary in order to compensate for the self-created suffering of our everyday life, which we experience as mundane and constricting. To simply be a human being living a spontaneous and balanced life is a notion that we tend to resist. This is not to say that there are not "extraordinary" experiences that may be experienced, that will occur, as and when they occur, but they are not in and of themselves Truth, Awakening and Freedom.

So I hope that what I have shared in this book has convinced you that you do not have to go and sit in a cave for years, or recite a mantra, or become a monk or nun, to ignite and burn up in the Fire of the Heart. You do not necessarily have to renounce your profession, your relationships or your family life. You simply cannot know in advance what the Fire of the Heart will demand of you, so simply live and embrace all that is arising in your life right *now* as your Path, in the context of the ever-present Goal of True Happiness, Peace, Freedom and Fulfillment here and now, and see what comes.

Our challenge is not just to see and feel this potential but to *live* it. It is to become a truly *human* being, an *extra-ordinary*, human being, who is *lived* by the Mystery that is already animating everything. By "extra-ordinary" I do not mean that we become mundane or mediocre. I mean that we begin to function as a human being that *knows* that they are being lived by a greater Being, a greater Power. When we function as conscious human beings we can be marvelous, intensely creative people. Then our activity is not engaged in the strife of seeking and resisting, it is simply a spontaneous expression and celebration of a life already lived in Truth. Our ever-deepening Awakened Life will be a life of enjoyment, of communion, of celebration, of becoming evermore intelligent, sensitive and loving under all conditions.

We will welcome the purifying demand of the Fire of the Heart. It will hurt like hell at times. It will throw us into confusion. It will show us our foolishness. It will create friction. It will confront us with all the crazy things about ourselves. It will offend our self-images, and it will force us to function humanly in spite of our refusal to function. But, after all, that is what we are all here to face, embrace and purify, isn't it? What else is there to do here? Every obstacle, challenge or block that appears to be in our way *is* The Way. In the Awakening Process all that we hold onto, gross or subtle, all that we defend, all that we contract around, in our insistence on some sense of independent self-existence, is progressively undermined, broken down, and ultimately seen and felt through. Just as rivers are swallowed up by the ocean, so all of our lesser ways must lead eventually to the Great Way. Social moralities, beliefs, customs and doctrines, matter little, for all that *truly* matters is that the Extraordinary and the Extra-ordinary become the norm.

The more unflinchingly we face our unconsciousness, our fear, our attachments, and all the strategies and games of our ego "I" without reacting, then the more we understand ourselves, the more we see through our refusal to love, the more we discover essential *simplicity.* That simplicity is the acceptance of responsibility for being what we *are.* It is to have the will and the Pure Passion, to live life unafraid to *be* Life. It is to be what we are from moment to moment without pretense, to care deeply about Life and all others, without worrying about what others think of us.

Through devoting ourselves to a sincere practice of True Meditation, through staying receptive to the innocence of Wide Open Wonder, through trusting in the guidance of the Power That Knows The Way, and through surrendering ourselves to the Fire of the Heart, everything that is false, fleeting and insubstantial is burned to ash, leaving only That, which is *always already* the case – the inherent Happiness, Love, Peace and Freedom, that is the very essence of Life and Consciousness Itself, forever shining forth *now* and *now* and *now.*

# Epilogue

MEDITATION is not what you think. True Meditation *always already* IS! Whether you are thinking or not thinking, whether you are aware of it or not, Consciousness Itself is eternally meditating the entire universe, and all the other billions of universes and beings.

Take it All The Way and True Meditation is not just a practice that you engage in, it seeps into every corner of your Life and Being. It becomes YOU. It takes the little "you" over. It subsumes you. It sublimes you. It transfigures you.

Let this in. Pure Being is enveloping you *right now*. Pure Being *is* YOU right now. Your body-mind and the entire world and universe are floating in YOU!

Let go of all limiting content and merge into limitless Context. All phenomena are intrinsically empty, yet this Consciousness, that they are identical with, is not mere nothingness. It does exist, but in a way that is too marvelous and miraculous for you to comprehend. It is an Existence that is beyond Existence, a Non-Existence that is nevertheless Existence.

Being Consciousness, Being Meditation, is being in the world, but not of it. Resting as Prior Unity, as Eternity in Love with the productions of time, you are *always already* Free of what arises. Where is the "you" that has a connection to it? There is no connection. There is no "you" to find.

There is Di-vine Communion Only – Being *and* Becoming, Transcendent *and* Immanent, Heaven *and* Earth, fused as ONE Indivisible Whole, that does not stand in relationship to anything. There is no difference between the Divine and the arising of phenomena. Nothing intervenes.

*At the level of Pure Existence*

*Mystery prevails.*

*Soaked in the Infinite Ocean*

*Of staggering*

*Wild*

*Kaleidoscopic*

*Multidimensional Mystery,*

*This incandescent fluid Beauty*

*Of now-naked Life,*

*You are Radiant*

*With the knit of Identity*

*And the humming of unseen harps.*

*Be Consciousness*

*Burn in the Great Fire*

*And all conditions of experience*

*All thoughts*

*Are transcended.*

*In every instant*

*The search falls away*

*There is only the sacrifice of conditions*

*Into the Feeling of Infinity*
*Into the Fire of the Heart.*

*Soon the transparency of everything*
*Dissolves everything*
*In unreasonable Joy.*

*So Be It!*

*Love is the key we must turn*
*Truth is the flame we must burn*
*Freedom the lesson we must learn*
*Do you know what I mean?*
*Have your eyes really seen?*


*Lesley Ann Cox*

# Bibliography

Adi Da Samraj –

The Knee of Listening, The Dawn Horse Press, 1972

The Method of the Siddhas, The Dawn Horse Press, 1973

The Enlightenment of the Whole Body, The Dawn Horse Press, 1978

(Original versions in the name of Bubba Free John)

The Ancient Walkabout Way, The Dawn Horse Press, 2007


Aurobindo, Sri –

The Synthesis of Yoga, Sri Aurobindo Ashram, 1948

The Psychic Being, Sri Aurobindo Ashram, 1989


Cohen, Andrew –

My Master Is Myself, Moksha Press, 1989

Evolutionary Enlightenment, Select Books, 2011


Harding, Douglas – On Having No Head, Arkana, 1986


Khantipalo, Phra – Buddhism Explained, Phra Mahamkut Rajavidyalaya
Press, 1988


Long, Barry – Only Fear Dies, Barry Long Books, 1986

Maharshi, Ramana – Be Who You Are, Edited by David Godman, Arkana, 1985

Nisagardatta Maharaj, Sri – I Am That, Chetana, 1973

Ragnar, Peter – The Magic Man, Roaring Lion Publishing, 1990

Jae Jah Noe – Do you see what I see?, Quest, 1977

Spira, Rupert – The Nature of Consciousness, New Harbinger, 2017

Suzuki, Shunryu – Zen Mind, Beginner's Mind, 1970

Trungpa, Chogyam – Cutting Through Spiritual Materialism, Shambhala, 1973

Watts, Alan W. - The Wisdom of Insecurity, Pantheon, 1953

Wilber, Ken –
Integral Meditation, Shambhala, 2016
A Brief History of Everything, Shambhala, 1997

# About the Author

ORIGINALLY from England, Peter studied English Literature in London and then, inspired by his longing for spiritual freedom, spent many years traveling the world. He participated in many intensive meditation retreats, and in monastic life in the Theravada Forest Tradition in the Western lineage of Ajahn Chah, where he experienced his initial Awakening and almost became a Buddhist monk. His trajectory abruptly changed course in 1992, when he had a profound Awakening to the radical immediacy of Freedom here and now, through reading the Advaita Vedanta classic I Am That by Sri Nisagardatta Maharaj. This Awakening was magnified when he soon after met the fiery young American spiritual teacher, Andrew Cohen. He was involved for the next thirteen years with the organization and spiritual community EnlightenNext, in a radical and progressive experiment in evolutionary enlightenment, based primarily in the United States. In 2007, after two years of intensive retreat on the island of Ibiza, Spain, while living on a permaculture farm, he and his new partner Cynthia bought the abandoned mountain farm of Quinta da Mizarela in Central Portugal, and co-founded The Awakened Life Project.

Besides being a spiritual guide to the growing international network of students involved with The Awakened Life Project, Peter teaches retreats and courses that catalyze Awakening to the radical immediacy of Freedom here and now, and facilitate the transformational task of embodying that Realization in everyday life. He has a keen interest in men's development, and has led a committed men's group for many years. A great lover of Portugal and the Portuguese, he founded the initiative "EvoLusa: For a more Awakened Portugal", to illuminate the underappreciated strengths and potentials he sees in the Portuguese character.

In 2017 Peter embarked on a spiritual pilgrimage in India and experienced a profound deepening through the Grace of Ramana Maharshi, while meditating in Virupaksha cave on Arunachala mountain, where Ramana had lived in silence in his early years. Peter has also experienced a profound and ever-deepening Recognition-Response to the Teaching and Divine Grace of Avatar Adi Da Samraj.

Peter's other interests include playing blues guitar, practicing qi gong, hiking on the mountain trails surrounding Quinta da Mizarela, foraging for wild edibles, exploring and exposing the lies we have been told about just about everything, and a nice cup of tea and a sit down.

For more information about The Awakened Life Project:

www.awakenedlifeproject.org

For articles, audios, videos, retreats and courses with Peter Bampton:

www.thefireoftheheart.com

Printed in Great Britain
by Amazon

33355516R00210